"*I don't know a wiser, more gracious wor*
I could listen to her forever!"

Beth Moore, founder of Living Proof Ministries,
author of fifteen books, conference speaker,
Bible study teacher, and radio host

"*The quality and integrity in which this book is written is only surpassed
by Lois Evans's life. In this must-read book, Lois creatively uses mentors
and the Word of God to challenge us to remember the personal faithfulness of God through every moment, second, minute, hour, and day of our
lives. Everyone who reads this book and takes it to heart will be forever
changed to overcome any rock-hard place with unmovable rock-hard
faith.*"

Thelma Wells, president of A Woman of God Ministries,
founder of Daughters of Zion Leadership Mentoring
Program (Mama T)

Joshua speaks of stones of remembrance,

"*In the future when your descendants ask their fathers, 'What do
these stones mean? Tell them . . . the* LORD *your God did to the
Jordan just what he had done to the Red Sea when he dried it up before us until we had crossed over. He did this so that all the peoples of
the earth might know that the hand of the* LORD *is powerful and so
that you might always fear the Lord your God.*" *(Joshua 4:19–24)*

*The body of Christ is like living stones, being built into a spiritual house
to be a holy priesthood, offering spiritual sacrifices acceptable to God
through Jesus Christ. For in Scripture it says:*

"*See, I lay a stone in Zion, a chosen and precious cornerstone,
and the one who trusts in him and will never be put to shame.*" *Now
to you who believe, this stone is precious. (1 Peter 2:6–7)*

Lois Evans brilliantly gathers stones of remembrance of God's miracle-working power in the lives of believers. Her keen insight into the heritage of a child of God enables the reader to cling to the hope that Christ, our Blessed Hope, will deliver them from despair and take them to victory as we consider that in every life there is a time of commemoration of what God has done for His children.

There is a time for everything, and a season for every activity under heaven: a time to be born and a time to die, a time to plant and a time to uproot . . . a time to scatter stones and a time to gather them . . . a time to be silent and a time to speak. (Ecclesiastes 3:5, 7)

As you read this life-changing book, think of the stones of remembrance in your own life and give testimony to God's miraculous intervention for if we keep quiet of who the Lord is, then Jesus, our Savior, promises that the "stones will cry out" of His majesty.
Diana Hagee, chief of staff for John Hagee Ministries

"This book is both powerful and challenging. It is a spiritual compass for all women who desire a navigation tool during the flood-stages of their lives. It will help a person to critically think through some of the same issues that our Old Testament girlfriends faced! It is a pleasure to read and would be an important addition to any Christian woman's library."
Vonette Bright, cofounder of Campus Crusade for Christ

Stones of Remembrance *is a masterpiece of tapestry weaving familiar and unfamiliar Old Testament female personalities with the threads of God's word, prayer, transparency, and emotional healing into the fabrics of every contemporary woman's life. Authentic tapestries are stretched by the weaver vertically and horizontally. The reader will emerge as a changed woman beautifying her surroundings as the Weaver loops the lessons taught until they become lessons lived.*
Shelia M. Bailey, president of E.K. Bailey Ministries, Inc.

LOIS EVANS
with JANE RUBIETTA

STONES OF REMEMBRANCE
A ROCK-HARD FAITH FROM ROCK-HARD PLACES

MOODY PUBLISHERS
CHICAGO

Cover Design: Terry Dugan Design
Cover Images: Indexstock /Alamy
Editor: Ali Diaz

Library of Congress Cataloging-in-Publication Data

Evans, Lois, 1949-
    Stones of remembrance : a rock-hard faith from rock-hard places / by Lois Evans with Jane Rubietta.
        p. cm.
    Includes bibliographical references.
    ISBN-13: 978-0-8024-8398-0
    1. Women in the Bible—Study and teaching. 2. Bible. O.T.—Biography—Study and teaching. I. Rubietta, Jane. II. Title.
BS575.E93 2006
220.9'2082—dc22

2006021420

ISBN: 0-8024-8398-4
ISBN-13: 978-0-8024-8398-0

We hope you enjoy this book from Moody Publishers. Our goal is to provide high-quality, thought-provoking books and products that connect truth to your real needs and challenges. For more information on other books and products written and produced from a biblical perspective, go to www.moodypublishers.com or write to:

Moody Publishers
820 N. LaSalle Boulevard
Chicago, IL 60610

1 3 5 7 9 10 8 6 4 2

Printed in the United States of America

Stones of Remembrance
is dedicated with love and gratitude

To my mother and grandmother,
who lived out the blessings
of remembering God's goodness and faithfulness,
and to the the other ladies who have taught me to remember.
—Lois Evans

To the women who courageously
choose to hold fast to God
in rock-hard places.
—Jane Rubietta

CONTENTS

Memory Stone

I remember the days of old;
I meditate on all Your works;
I muse on the work of Your hands. . . .
My soul longs for You like a thirsty land.

— *Psalm 143:5-6*

$\mathcal{I}$NTRODUCTION

$\mathcal{T}$hink about your day. Your yesterday. The circumstances swirling about you: relationships, job, finances, worries about the future, regrets over the past. Wherever you are today, whatever is happening in your life today, is not new to the human experience. The God we serve did not come into existence when we decided to make Him Lord, but He has been here from eternity past, and has all power to take care of your situation and mine. In *Stones of Remembrance,* we want to be encouraged and reminded that God is in the process of bringing us to maturity in Him. His blending-machine process is to mix all things together for good. His good, our good.

Sometimes situations come up in my life, and all I have is His Word. The fact of the matter is that God let this circumstance pass through His hands. Don't you think, then, that the Lord has a plan, and He wants us to rest in Him? We can learn to enter His rest by remembering who He is and what He has done for us, taking a look at His track record. In the busyness of our lives, we need to make adjustments to remember the goodness of the Lord. We witness this repeatedly in the Scriptures. We have to get back to the Word, because when all else fails, you belong to the "good hands" Person. Jesus never fails. He is the same yesterday, today, and He will be the same forever.

As a child growing up with seven siblings, even with a lack of conveniences, lack of money, and lack of support, I remember my mother and grandmother telling me about the goodness of God. We lived on Dad's income alone, and there were stretching times. But I also remember rich sessions around my mother's knees as she taught us the Word in our devotions every day.

After my grandfather died, I remember my grandmother carrying on with dignity and grace, living with limited resources; but always love, stories, and food abounded. This is God's specialty: He can take just what you have and make it much. They had confidence that He could provide over and over again.

Could it be that because we already have so much, we have difficulty finding time to focus on what is ultimately important? Are we focusing more on the benefits than on the benefit Giver? He wants us to remember in the good times and the bad times that He is good.

God wants to take us back to remember His goodness. Remembering will keep us focused in those times when it seems like He has forgotten us. You could be in the Word daily, praying daily, doing all the right things; and life still falls apart. The natural question is *why*—or should it be *who?* Who holds the key to open these prison gates and unlock these chains of frustration, depression, disillusionment, despair? I want to challenge you today to make your total focus the Word of God, and as a way of life, remember what He has done.

Stones of Remembrance takes us back to our sisters in the Bible who pressed through a number of challenges. I know you might be thinking, *That was then; this is the twenty-first century.* However, we need to remember that we are dealing with the "I AM" God who never changes. And you'll find that these women, who lived during the Exodus and the settling of the Promised Land, faced many of the same issues we do. Their stories freshen our faith and bring us into new places of courage and healing in the rock-hard spots of our lives.

*G*etting the Most from *Stones of Remembrance*

Stones of Remembrance is designed for easy use for your spiritual and emotional growth and health. It can be read one chapter at a time or a few pages at a time. *Stones* is also intended for use in discipling, counseling, accountability, and small group relationships. Each chapter contains sections for application and group discussion. To help facilitate women's gatherings, special features are included to spark heart conversation and bypass surface small talk. Our hope is that *Stones of Remembrance* will bring you, our sisters, more deeply to God's heart, and that your faith will be built up as you remember God's faithfulness in the lives of our Old Testament girlfriends, as well as in your own personal life.

In *Stones of Remembrance,* you'll find these special features:

Memory Stone

This Scripture encapsulates the key theme of the chapter, and works as a memory verse. The more Scripture flowing through our veins and the more Scripture we can call to mind, the better able we are to remember God's faithfulness, to remember God's nature, and to hold on in hard times to His truth.

Travel Mercies

The chapters close with five key questions that might be asked by a godly friend, mentor, or counselor; these can be used as journaling starters or in small groups. While the stories of the women in the Scriptures are informative for their own sakes, we hope that their lives make a difference in our lives, for Jesus' sake. Travel Mercies will help us transfer the concepts from the women's lives to our own situation and life.

What Mean These Stones?

The Israelites remembered God's faithfulness every time they viewed stones piled in a stack after a particular event. This section offers a commitment, a promise; here you say, "I will do this, tell this story, remember that event." We honor God's work in our lives and share that blessing with others in this portion.

Power Up

This passage from the Word allows us to apply truth to the facts of our life. Use it to memorize, to meditate, or to contemplate. You might write it on an index card and carry it with you, inviting God to continue to speak into your heart His truth in the midst of confounding and complex circumstances and relationships.

Rock-Hard Truth

Whether classic or contemporary, this quote comes from someone who knows the hard places in life, affirming our journey thus far and our hope in the God who holds the future in His hands.

Remember Me, O Lord

Read this closing prayer with your eyes and heart open toward the Lord, inviting Him to consolidate His work in your life and continue to encourage and strengthen you.

SMALL GROUP SUGGESTIONS

As you use *Stones of Remembrance* in your group, here are various possibilities that make facilitation simple and stress-free. You don't have to use all the portions in each session; feel free to pick and choose those which seem most relevant for your group. Beware, though, some of the sections may at first feel uncomfortable—don't miss God's good intentions for community, hope, and healing by shying away from temporary discomfort in the group setting.

1. Open your time together with a prayer, and then recite the "Memory Stone" text aloud, together. In Israel, believers stand anytime the Scriptures are read. This physical response to God's Word creates a spiritual response in our souls.

2. Appoint someone to read a pulled-out quote aloud and invite discussion from group members. Do this with other pulled-out quotes until reaching the "Travel Mercies" section.

3. Read each question in the "Travel Mercies" section out loud, creating room for individuals to answer. Don't be afraid of silence as women think, or as they try to gather courage to share something painful. Don't try to solve their problems or answer every question, but allow feelings and stories to arise naturally, giving women the freedom to talk, weep, grieve, or wonder aloud about God.

4. "What Mean These Stones?" becomes a place of commitment: here is what I will do; this is the story I will tell. So welcome your women into that commitment by asking those questions.

5. For "Power Up," read the verse as a group and then wait in silence for God to speak individually to the members. Then ask the group to talk about their application of the Scripture: What does that passage mean to you? How does it apply in your life? What is God saying to you?

6. Consider "Rock-Hard Truth" with an eye toward individual relevance.

7. Together, say aloud the prayer in "Remember Me, O Lord." You might stand, joining hands to signify your circle of friendship and your covenant to stand together with one another in the hard places of life.

Whether in times of solitude or with a group of women clustered about you, as you stack your stones of remembrance, may you draw on the mighty presence and power of God, the Rock of your salvation. Though your circumstances may be difficult and your struggles monumental, though your relationships may seem hopeless or crumbling, God will never fail. May His peace be your power.

Memory Stone

"He is the Rock,
His work is perfect;
For all His ways are justice,
A God of truth and without injustice;
Righteous and upright is He."

— *Deuteronomy 32:4*

CHAPTER ONE

SETTING STONES
IN PLACE

The glass in the windows rattled as her daughter stormed from the house, slamming the front door. Anne wondered which would break first: her heart or her daughter's rebellion. In a face-off with God, Anne stretched out on the floor of her bedroom, facing the ceiling. After the racking sobs subsided, she began to think back two, three years.

Her first child too wreaked havoc on their lives and himself as he struggled to find his own way. Eventually, with a mighty shove of the Holy Spirit, her son had squeezed through his self-made torture chamber and into the freedom of life in Christ.

Remembering her son, remembering God's faithfulness in that situation, Anne began to believe that God would be faithful with her daughter. She could hold on and trust Him. He had proven Himself over and over.

Remembering

Through her pain, Anne discovered an age-old truth about God, and about the faith process. In the midst of distress and difficulty, God is faithful, because He cannot be anything less. The process of remembering those very acts by a faithful God brought Anne into a place of renewed hope. And faith.

How often do the circumstances of our lives threaten to cut our hearts in half? And how often have we found that the Lord is faithful to see us through, if we will only hold on and continue to call on God's reputation?

In Scripture, the Lord tells us repeatedly, "Remember." Perhaps my favorite place in the Bible that talks about remembering is Joshua 3 and 4. After four hundred years of slavery in Egypt, and then forty years of desert wandering, the Israelites stood at the cusp of the Promised Land, on the edge of their future. They had been waiting for this moment since Abraham's time. Only a teeny issue separated them from walking into the homeland God had promised for many years: a river.

But not just any river. This was the River Jordan, and the Israelites stared as turbulent waters raged past them. Waters at flood stage overflowed the banks of the river, eating away at the shoreline, running in rivulets toward them.

Joshua halted their fear and called on the faith of the children of Israel. He said, "And it shall come to pass, as soon as the soles of the feet of the priests who bear the ark of the Lord, the Lord of all the earth, shall rest in the waters of the Jordan, that the waters of the Jordan shall be cut off, the waters that come down from upstream, and they shall stand as a heap"(3:13).

The priests stepped out, and it was so. The waters peeled back and rose up in a pile upstream, and nearly two million people, their livestock, and caravans crossed over the river on dry ground. Not muddy, soggy ground, but dry ground. From floods and mud to dry dirt and millions of footsteps walking into freedom. God does not take halfway measures—not then, not now.

After the crossing, the Lord said to Joshua, "Take for yourselves twelve men from the people, one man from every tribe, and command them, saying, 'Take for yourselves twelve stones from here, out of the midst of the Jordan, from the place where the priests' feet stood firm. You shall carry them over with you and leave them in the lodging place where you lodge tonight'" (4:2–3).

> *The stones set in place a rock-hard
> faith from rock-hard places.*

Each of the chosen priests hefted a huge stone and hauled it from the riverbed to the new camp in the new land. These stones would serve as a marker, a signpost among the people, so that "when your children ask in time to come, saying, 'What do these stones mean to you?' Then you shall answer them that the waters of the Jordan were cut off before the ark of the covenant of the Lord; when it crossed over the Jordan, the waters of the Jordan were cut off. And these stones shall be for a memorial to the children of Israel forever" (4:6–7).

Remembering God's might and faithfulness would see Israel through rough waters and tough crossings. Remembering becomes a tool that sees us through present pain and difficulties and propels us into new, faith-filled spaces, preparing us for the future.

Rock-Hard Faith

The stones from the Israelites' journey across the Jordan River served as a faith trigger for them, and for the generations that followed. The stones reminded them of God's power yesterday, last week, last year. Every time they saw the stones, they remembered God's faithfulness, God's strength, God's mighty love and strong hand of deliverance. The stones set in place a rock-hard faith from rock-hard places. The memorial reminded them, over and over, that their faithful God could and would deliver again and again.

We all have our Jordan Rivers, where the waters roil and our faith quakes and we are barricaded from passing through into victory. Peg and Bob's river extended to their whole family. Each time one of their daughters called and announced a new life stirring within her, they rejoiced and could scarcely wait to share the news with everyone they knew. When their youngest daughter, the last of their childless children, called to announce she was finally pregnant, they threw caution and good sense to the wind. They rushed out even before the blue pregnancy-test strip was dry to purchase chenille blankets, fleecy pajamas, and cuddly toys.

But in a matter of weeks, their joy turned to caution when their daughter called to say that she'd experienced spotting. The doctor suggested an early ultrasound. Then a blood test. He assured them, however, that all seemed fine. "Sometimes this just happens," the doctor said. Eager to believe, the entire family carefully counted the weeks for her first trimester to be completed—a time after which they would surely be into the safety zone.

But, two weeks before arriving at this milestone, an early morning call shattered the quiet and their hopes. Their daughter sobbed into the phone. "Mom, I've been at the hospital all night. We lost the baby."

A close family, the entire clan converged on the daughter's home to mingle their tears, exchange hugs, and talk out their sorrow. Something beautiful was gone forever. No well-meaning words by friends, who assured them that more children would come, could erase the pain of the loss of this child who was promised and so lovingly expected.

During that trying time, Peg's daughter and her husband experienced not only a barrenness of the womb, but also a barrenness of spirit. Their hope and joy faded, and months passed before they could begin to dream that maybe, just maybe, God would bless them with another child. Barrenness of spirit became a daunting floodplain in the lives of several family members.

These moments when the well of your soul is empty—these are the times when you need to remember God's power and the times in the past when He has sustained you.

$\mathcal{A}$ Flooding Fear

Early in our marriage, Tony traveled frequently, which meant I was home with young children. Fear riddled me in the night. I worried constantly about Tony's safety. Frequently I slept with the lights on. Finally I decided to turn my devotional life into a study of deliverance from my fear, using Psalm 34 steadily until I learned to trust the Lord completely in this area. I began to arm myself with Scriptures, memorizing and quoting repeatedly, "I sought the Lord, and He heard me, and delivered me from all my fears. . . . The angel of the Lord encamps all around those who fear Him, and delivers them" (Psalm 34:4, 7).

When my (Jane) children were young, I prayed Scripture over them at bedtime to combat nighttime fears. Whether they were awakening with bad dreams or afraid to go to sleep, I would wrap them in my arms and recite God's words over them. As the children got older and were more resistant to such overt touch and faith, I simply laid my hand on them and claimed the words and the truth silently. Sometimes while they slept, I stood by their beds and covered them in Scripture prayers. Favorites include Philippians 2:9–11; 4:6–8; Romans 8:31–39; 2 Timothy 1:7. Even now, we both still pray Scriptures over those we love. Sometimes we pray silently, sometimes when gently patting or touching, always trying to communicate peace and Christ's presence in places of anxiety or fear.

Perhaps your flood stage comes through financial duress. Possibly it is a broken or breaking marriage, an unfaithful spouse, a prodigal child, parenting your grandchildren. Or maybe you have never married and still scan the horizon for the man of your dreams, and meanwhile battle a broken heart over your singleness. Perhaps your current crisis involves job loss, or underemployment, or discrimination, or problems with your health, or infertility.

Fear is natural in the floodplains of our lives.

But fear is no match for God. He creates goodness out of grotesque situations, and in the midst of our Jordan River, we remember where the Lord has delivered us in the past. These memories are souvenir stones of God's faithfulness. God can part the waters, God can dry the riverbed, God can make a way for us. He has done it before.

He can do it again. These are the instances we call to mind. These moments reinstall our faith and reboot our hope and empower us to set foot into the water.

Remembering as an act of faith
negates the fear that holds us hostage.

Imagine, as the Hebrew people gawked and shuffled about at the banks of the Jordan, what stories began to whisper through their minds and then back and forth to one another. Stories of plagues, of frogs and bloody water and locusts and the death fog; stories of Egyptians hard on their heels as they escaped to the desert, of a cloud by day and a fire by night; stories of another body of water, the Red Sea, and the miraculous splitting of those waters; stories of another crossing on dry ground. Stories of a faithful God, the one true God, the God who had delivered them in the past. These stories called forth faith in the followers of Yahweh, faith that allowed them to step forward into the future promised long ago.

*T*he Stories in the Stones

Are you facing a river too full and wild to cross? God wants to tether us to His side during the turbulent times in our lives. He longs to build into us qualities of endurance. In the midst of circumstances that we might not choose, our Lord may not deliver us from the situation. But He can certainly set us free in the midst of the problems and pain.

In our journey together through *Stones of Remembrance*, we will explore various women in Scripture who were used by God to accomplish His good purposes. Through their struggles and their faith, we will remember the God who makes a way for us in the teeming rivers of our lives.

This will be an archaeological dig of sorts. We will excavate the lives of women in the Scriptures, and excavate our own lives as well. As we unearth our stones, gently brushing off the stories from our past that display God's faithfulness, we will be encouraged and our faith will grow. These stones of remembrance lay a foundation on which God longs to build us into mighty women, just as Peter says: "You also, as living stones, are being built up a spiritual house, a holy priesthood" (1 Peter 2:5).

The Purposes of God's Memory Stones

Challenges and issues in the past and present can hold us hostage. Are there situations in your life that you will not let go—you bring them up time and time again? They become an excuse to camp on the wrong side of the river. As one pastor's wife wrote, "My childhood has hung around much too long and now I am getting free."

Don't be like the elephants at the circus. They are trained to stand still and be in bondage. A baby elephant is chained to a peg in the dirt with a cuff around its ankle. The chain takes away willpower, so by adulthood an elephant has no idea that its strength far surpasses the strength of the feeble peg in the ground. So these mighty beasts —whose grandparents likely once thundered through plains in a land of freedom, far, far away—stand docilely attached to a flimsy chain.

We too have been trained by our old master, Satan, but at the cross we were set free. Jesus tells us, "Therefore if the Son makes you free, you shall be free indeed" (John 8:36). Thanks be to God, who wants to break those chains so that we can walk in freedom into the Promised Land.

God's purposes in stones of remembrance become even more apparent as our lives and stones and stories impact the lives of those around us. It was true in Joshua's River Jordan dilemma, and it is true for our dilemmas now. "The Lord your God dried up the waters of the Jordan before you until you had crossed over, as the Lord your God did to the Red Sea, which He dried up before us until we had crossed over, that all the peoples of the earth may know the hand of the Lord, that it is mighty, that you may fear the Lord your God forever" (Joshua 4:23–24).

The rocks of remembering call to mind the hardships of our journey and the Lord's deliverance. To all who come near our lives, they serve as a testimony of God's goodness and power. For Joshua and his desert conquerors, the Lord answered this prayer immediately:

> So it was, when all the kings of the Amorites who were on the west side of the Jordan, and all the kings of the Canaanites who were by the sea, heard that the Lord had dried up the waters of the Jordan from before the children of Israel until we had crossed over, that their heart melted; and there was no spirit in them any longer because of the children of Israel (Joshua 5:1).

When the Israelites summoned their courage by remembering God's power and then surging forward, the stories of their deliverance spread. Their enemies dissolved before them, and the Hebrew children conquered the land the Lord had pledged to them since Abraham's time.

We need stones of remembrance because of the challenges awaiting us in the future. The Enemy plans to fight against us—but "He who is in you is greater than he who is in the world" (1 John 4:4). We too can conquer the land the Lord gives us. We can and will see the mighty hand of the Lord displaying His power and purpose to those around us as we remember and move forward. But this requires preparation on our part: we need to expect God to show up and be ready for the miracle.

*P*reparing Our Hearts

Just as bodybuilders pump iron to get ready for their next strength event, we get ready for God to act by pumping up on Scripture. God primed Joshua for success with these words: "This Book of the Law shall not depart from your mouth, but you shall meditate in it day and night, that you may observe to do according to all that is written in it. For then you will make your way prosperous, and then you will have good success" (Joshua 1:8).

A friend who served in the army said, "We were given a black book. It contained all the specifics and directions. We were to carry the book with us at all times, so that if we had questions and no one was available to answer them, we could look in the book. We slept with the book by our side, and if we were caught without the black book, we dropped to the floor for push-ups."

Our black book is the Bible. Carry the Word of God in your heart and in your hand. Don't be caught without it. Like the priests who stepped into the water, carrying the ark of the covenant in front of them. The results will change the trajectory of your life, and transform both you and those you intercept. Charles Spurgeon said:

Never, never neglect the word of God; that will make thy heart rich with precept, rich with understanding; and then thy conversation, when it flows from thy mouth, will be like thine heart, rich, unctuous and savory. Make thy heart full of rich, generous love, and then the stream that flows from thy hand will be just as rich and generous as thine heart. Oh! go, Christian, to the great mine of riches, and cry unto the Holy Spirit to make thy heart rich unto salvation. So shall thy life and conversation be a boon to thy fellows; and when they see thee, thy face shall be as the angel of God.[1]

Our success doesn't hinge on what the culture at-large says or does, or how others act toward us, or even on the outcome of our circumstances. Our ultimate success totally depends on God: God's Son the living Word, and God's written Word in us, filling us, directing us. And then, when we come to our River Jordan, the Word swells up within us and we remember, and find hope, and are able to move forward into success. Success on God's terms.

Real success requires a habit of moving into the secret place with God (Psalm 91). Along with our black book, meditating on the Word day and night, we also prepare for God to act by purifying our hearts. Joshua gathered the Hebrew people and said, "Sanctify yourselves, for tomorrow the Lord will do wonders among you" (Joshua 3:5). Joshua expected God to do amazing feats because he had filled his mind with God's presence and His Word—and then he prepared himself and his soldiers. They were expected to be free of sin so that their holy God could appear among them and lead them out into battle.

So often we have three strikes against us before we even step out: we don't expect God to do wonders among us, we don't fill and feast our hearts on the Scriptures, and we run about the camp with impure hearts. We get in the way of God's work. The psalmist said, "Search me, O God, and know my heart; try me, and know my anxieties; and see if there is any wicked way in me, and lead me in the way everlasting" (Psalm 139:23–24).

When we get ready for God to act, we can be certain He will do it. Just remember: He has done it before. He can do it again and again and again.

WHAT TO DO WHEN
YOU DON'T KNOW WHAT TO DO
Wait silently (Psalm 62:5).
Pour out your heart (Psalm 62:8).
Trust in Him at all times (Proverbs 3:5–8).
Cling to the rock (Psalm 18:46).

Crossing Over Our Jordan Rivers

We don't know when God will get us over the river. We don't know how God will dry the riverbed and allow us to cross. But we do know, by faith, that He will act on our behalf. And while we wait, we remember.

❖ We remember our Red Seas, the places where God has parted the waters for us, the impossible places where God came through and the Enemy was defeated.

❖ We remember who brought us through.

❖ We remember whose we are. We belong to Christ!

❖ We remember that God's delays are not delays of in-activity, but of preparation. He delays, but He does not deny. While we wait He prepares us for His answer according to His perfect, preordained plan.

❖ We remember and link up with like-minded, stronger people who are going in the same direction. We can't afford to attempt the waters of the Jordan alone.

❖ We remember to tell our children, and our children's children, that they may see the mighty hand of God and take courage for the rivers they will have to cross. They piggyback on our faith when we share the stories of God's mighty acts in our lives.

❖ We remember to offer encouragement for our friends (Hebrews 10:24–25; 2 Corinthians 1:3–4).

Moving On

Remembering is good. But we can't just reminisce about God's goodness. The children of Israel could have just talked about the Red Sea wonders while standing at the Jordan River, and it would not have made any difference. Talk is cheap. They had to move into the new challenge, pulling on the strength of the past—pulling on God's strength. And His strength is perfect. His power is perfected in our weakness (2 Corinthians 12:9).

Ultimately, our remembering fuels our faith and we forge ahead. It's too easy to sit around, remembering, all the while increasing our inertia. At some point, we proclaim with Joshua, "Advance!" (6:7, NIV) and get a move on.

Because faith that does not act is a faith that is just an act.

Travel Mercies

1. Take note of where you are *right now*. Spiritually, emotionally, physically, relationally. Where is your faith being tested? Where is your River Jordan?

2. God set up stones on the bank of the Jordan both for the Israelites' obedience, and so the surrounding nations might know the power of God. Where is obedience required for you at this stage of your journey? Who around you is watching your life to see how God acts? Or to see if your faith is just an act?

3. When standing at the Jordan River, (1) we expect God to act, (2) we feast on God's Word, and (3) we purify our hearts before Him. When have you experienced God's hand in your life as a result of these kinds of preparations? Which of the three is hardest for you? Why?

4. What are your Red Seas? When has God displayed His power in your life in the *past*? What happens in your heart as you look back and remember, then look forward to your current fears and faith-tests?

5. How hard is it to share your Jordan River experiences with others? Who are the like-minded people with whom you contemplate these things? If you have not linked up with these companions, why not? How will you do that?

What Mean These Stones?

Choose some stones to stack: What would your stones of remembrance be, if you were to examine them today? What do you think your current trials mean for you spiritually? Invite God to bring hope into your heart for the burden you bear.

Power Up

"Don't for a minute let this Book of The Revelation be out of mind. Ponder and meditate on it day and night, making sure you practice everything written in it. Then you'll get where you're going; then you'll succeed. Haven't I commanded you? Strength! Courage! Don't be timid; don't get discouraged. God, your God, is with you every step you take."

—Joshua 1:8–9 THE MESSAGE

Rock-Hard Truth

"The king's efforts to destroy the strength of Israel —so clearly a work of God—met with failure again and again. And that failure was usually from the efforts of women, whom Pharaoh did not consider a threat."

—NET, note 60, Exodus 1:22

Remember Me, O Lord

Heavenly Father,
As I stand at the edge of my River Jordan,
I remember by faith the places
where You have dried up the Red Seas in my past.
I remember Your love and faithfulness
and I choose, now, to stack those stones of faith.
You will go before me. You have done it before.
I give You this day, the mud and floods in front of me,
and wait while You dry up the riverbed.
Amen.

Memory Stone

"And now, Israel,
what does the Lord your God
require of you,
but to fear the Lord your God,
to walk in all His ways
and to love Him,
to serve the Lord your God
with all your heart and with all your soul,
and to keep the commandments of the Lord
and His statutes which I command you today
for your good?"

— Deuteronomy 10:12-13

CHAPTER TWO

PUAH AND SHIPHRAH:

REMEMBERING THE FAITHFULNESS OF GOD

Tracy listened to the message on the recorder again. "Hey, Tracy, this is Jason. I'd love to take you out on Friday night. Give me a call back." During their few dates, she loved laughing and arguing current events with him, and found him intellectually her equal. But she quickly learned that he was not a believer. And he began pressuring her sexually.

At twenty-nine, she wondered if she would ever get married, if God would fulfill her heart's desires. Tracy called her friend and mentor. "Hold tight, Tracy," Renee said. "Remember this verse? 'The unmarried woman cares about the things of the Lord, that she may be holy both in body and in spirit' " (1 Corinthians 7:34).

After their conversation, Tracy listened silently before God, her heart on the altar. She remembered His Word; she remembered His holiness; she remembered that He has good plans for His children. Tracy remembered that she had to keep her eyes on Him so He could direct her paths, and she began to worship Him, right there in her living room.

Then she called Jason back—handsome, kind, but misled Jason—and explained that she loved the Lord so much, she couldn't continue a relationship with someone who didn't have a similar love for God. After hanging up the phone, Tracy wept, but felt deep down that she had done the right thing.

$\mathscr{T}$wo Uncompromising Women

Tracy, with Renee's encouragement, chose to honor the Lord, remembering His love for her and calling of her, in spite of her heart's longing to be married. She had to fight the lies in her head—lies that marketing and movies perpetuated—that she wasn't as valuable single, that sex outside of marriage made her acceptable and might secure a husband. But she feared, revered, and loved the Lord, and held fast in obedience.

Nearly lost in the compelling saga of the Israelites and their misery in Egypt are two women who also hold fast in obedience because of their fear of the Lord. Of the many faithful people playing vital roles in the annals of Hebrew history, only a few get press in the books. These two women are the first women mentioned in the Exodus accounting: the midwives Shiphrah and Puah.

In spite of the harsh labor, the brutal treatment endured at the hands of the Egyptians, the Hebrew slaves flourish. The nation within a nation grows so strong and mighty that the leadership becomes paranoid and threatened, and with good reason. Population growth —fertility—is viewed as a sign of blessing, and the Hebrew nation has grown exponentially during their years of forced servitude, from seventy people to several million. The "gods" are blessing the Israelites, and those very people might rebel and take over the host country.

The logical decision for Pharaoh is to order Shiphrah and Puah to slaughter all newborn boys. The Scriptures tell us, "But the midwives feared God, and did not do as the king of Egypt commanded them, but saved the male children alive" (Exodus 1:17).

When the king learns of their disobedience, he summons the midwives, demanding, "Why have you done this thing, and saved the male children alive?" (1:18).

They fear God. So they answer Pharaoh, the tyrant and slave driver of the Israelites, "Because the Hebrew women are not like the Egyptian women; for they are lively and give birth before the midwives come to them" (1:19).

The Lord honors their reverence of Him and resultant obedience to their calling. "Therefore God dealt well with the midwives, and the people multiplied and grew very mighty. And so it was, because the midwives feared God, that He provided households for them" (1:20–21). The Lord honors those who fear Him.

*W*hat's in a Name?

Considering how few major female players are listed in the Scriptures, it's awesome that the names of these two midwives are remembered and recorded, particularly in light of the meaning of their names. Shiphrah's name originates from the root word for *glisten*, and came to mean *splendid*, as in a tapestry or canopy, or a royal pavilion. Puah's name means "to glitter; brilliancy."[2]

Never underestimate the power of a woman who fears the Lord!

These are powerful descriptions, fitting of roles these women play in God's plans for Israel. Exodus literally means *ex odus*, a road out, and these two women shine with hope as they provide a way out for the Israelites by preserving the infant boys. These women will deliver and save the life of the man who will deliver a nation from bondage—Moses. Their fear of God sets in motion salvation for the world! Imagine the courage and conviction they possess as they choose to fear God rather than Pharaoh's death edicts. They save a nation from destruction, from systematic annihilation. Never underestimate the power of a woman who fears the Lord!

$\mathscr{R}$emembering Their God

What do they know about this God they feared, to display such radical faith and obedience? After all, He has been silent for most of the four hundred years in Egypt; no prophets spoke, no dreamers dreamed. In spite of the reverberating silence, the Hebrew midwives know the God who created the heavens and the earth. They know the One who sprinkled the night skies with stars and set them twinkling. They know the One who commands the sunrise and the sunset, who oversees the day and the night. They know the One who made man from the dust and a woman from his rib.

And they know what their parents and grandparents taught them about the one true God, stories handed down from generation to generation (Deuteronomy 6:6–9). They know the One who called Abraham when he was but one, and know the One who promised to make of that one man a mighty nation.

They remember the stories of a woman long past her prime, a woman whose old and shriveled womb refused to bear children until its fruit could only be declared a miracle. They know the stories of the son of that promise, Isaac on the altar and God's provision of a ram in the thicket to save his life. They remember that Abraham's obedience saved the life of his son, Isaac. They know the trickery of Jacob, his wrestling with the Lord, and of his name change, by God's grace, to Israel.

They exchange whispers of the God who spoke to Joseph in dreams, who turned evil into good by making of Joseph a great leader, who would provide sanctuary for the very family members who tried to kill him out of jealousy. They remember Joseph's promise to his brothers, "I am dying; but God will surely visit you, and bring you out of this land to the land of which He swore to Abraham, to Isaac, and to

Jacob" (Genesis 50:24). How can the Lord bring the Hebrew people out if the midwives kill all the boys?

Shiphrah and Puah know this God. And they bow their knees to Him, placing their lives in His hands and refusing to bow to a lower power than He. They know that they would die a slow soul death if they honor Pharaoh's death edict. These courageous women know the death sentence would be for their own hearts if they do not honor the God of all the universe over the ruler of the Egyptian empire.

They do not fear the one who had the power to take their earthly lives; they fear the One who had the power to take their eternal souls (see Matthew 10:28).

They remember and are awed by this God. And they deliver those babies.

As God blessed Shiphrah and Puah and the faithful Hebrews before them, He still blesses His children today. We remember His goodness, that He is trustworthy, that He has more than once delivered our friends and delivered us. Best of all, He never changes. Blessing comes in this life, and in eternity forever. While in those silent places, those desert-dry places where you wait for God to move, remember, in the desert the dew falls the freshest, and wait on the Lord (Isaiah 40:31). God's silence doesn't mean His absence. Just because you can't see or hear God doesn't negate His presence and active work behind the scenes. Base your movement on who you know and what you know about Him, not on what you are seeing and feeling at the moment.

$\mathcal{P}$utting Fear in Perspective

When Lynn gave birth to her first child, she says, "I remember thinking, *I am in a no-turning-back place. I can't worm my way out of this!* And I remember wanting my mother." What a universal longing in that place of fear. Lynn needed a Puah and Shiphrah in her life.

More than guiding the women through labor pains, teaching the early version of breathing and focusing, these brilliant, shining women also likely work with couples before marriage, coach them through pregnancy, and perhaps help with general health issues and infertility problems. They check the mother's health, the position and growth of the baby, watch for problems, listen for life, and prepare the women physically, emotionally, and spiritually for birth. They attend and minister in the crises of miscarriage, stillbirth, or the death of the mother in childbirth.

Shiphrah and Puah surely understand the connection between nature and nurture: that people living in harsh, abusive environments, likely with too little nutrition and with too much work, generally had low-birth-weight babies who might starve to death or die of childhood diseases before many years passed.

Yet these women witness the exact opposite. While their prowess might allow them to massage babies in the womb and turn a baby to prepare for proper birthing position,[3] their expertise cannot account for the postpartum flourishing of those babies. They watch them develop and thrive and the Hebrew contingent become a threat to the Egyptians. These midwives surely recognize the correlation between the birth of healthy babies and the blessing of God.

And they fear the God who can give life and take away life. They remembered the promise, handed down for generations: "I will multiply your descendants as the stars of the heaven and as the sand which is on the seashore. . ." (Genesis 22:17). They also know the other part of the promise: that suffering would be inevitable. But they have seen God's blessing on His people, who flourish in spite of hardship.

Witnessing the wonder of birth over and over must so impress them that they cannot toss into the Nile those squalling, scrunched-up miracles in whom breathes the very breath of God. Day after day Puah and Shiphrah saw life brought into wretched circumstances— squirming, wriggling, hungry life—and remember the promise of a future for their people. They know that the birth of a child is a sign that God wants the world to continue.

Living up to their names, Puah and Shiphrah form a canopy of protection over the future of Israel. They are a tapestry of brilliance, where God's holiness sparkles as He radiates life within them and through them.

Gauging Our Fear Levels

But how bright and shiny is the world today? We don't hear many good news reports these days. People don't know what to do with fear, whether defined as reverence or as a reaction to danger. Years ago, people lived in safer neighborhoods, didn't lock their doors at night, let their kids out to play in the morning and expected them home when the streetlights flicked on. And meanwhile, parents knew that children were out of harm's way, or that the neighbors would alert them if problems arose. Most people respected those in authority, people who made laws presumably for the good of the citizens.

Now we are a law unto ourselves, and create laws that reflect our wants and our sinful hearts rather than our fear of the Lord. We don't fear—respect—people in authority, whether it's the police or the school principal or the president of the United States. Instead, we fear people who have guns. We fear the gangs on the street. We fear people who can take our lives, or the lives of those we love. We fear those who can harm our children, or repossess our home or our car, or get us fired. We fear the person who knows some dirt about us and could smear our reputation. Fear riddles us, locks us in our houses, locks up our hearts, locks up our faith.

In the late nineties, a clothing company was born called *No Fear*, aimed at taking away our negative, self-limiting boundaries: fear of others, fear of heights, fear of risk. It refused to allow fear to be part of the athlete's equation, refused to allow fear to master or to determine one's participation in a sport—or in life, for that matter. It was hugely successful.

It is, however, not quite true in its slant. "No fear" living could easily be misinterpreted; it doesn't mean that we live foolishly, leaping off tall buildings without a safety net, taking senseless risks with our lives. We don't hurl ourselves into dangerous situations or relationships or activities just because we're trying to live "no fear" lives.

The first (and only) time that I (Jane) went rock climbing, I learned that the only way up that wall and back down was with a belayer, someone larger and stronger than I on the other end of the rope, keeping the line taut and keeping me stable, feeding more rope or tightening the rope as needed. Our actions always need ballast.

They need to be attached to a weight that will counter our own weight. A "no fear" society has lost the ballast, lost the counter-weight, lost the bigger and stronger Being who anchors us and keeps us stable.

We don't live in a generation that fears God, our ballast and be-layer. So when Proverbs 1:7 says, "The fear of the Lord is the begin-ning of knowledge," we shrug internally. We don't get it.

We sing "I love You," to the Lord, but we don't sing, "I fear You," or "I revere You," or even "I respect You." "Fear of God" sure isn't a category in the hymnals on my shelf.

We know facts about God. We can recite lists of His attributes, or a hundred names for Him, but we do not know how to live in those truths, nor how those characteristics pertain to our relationship with Him.

What we know about Puah and Shiphrah is that they fear God, and this changes the way they live. They answer to a power higher than the current pharaoh. They choose to put their hands and lives into the hands of the Holy God, the God of the promise, the God who said He would provide a road out, an *ex odus*.

How does remembering the fear of God work out in our lives?

Remembering the Fear of God

The fear of the Lord is not the same as the fear we understand. This is not the fear of a wife who is terrified of an abusive husband. This fear does not say, "I have to be perfect or you will leave me." Rather, this healthy revere-type fear is a lifestyle and attitude re-sponse to an assessment of another, a response that swells up within: admiration, love, respect in the highest form; an understanding of another's power and authority, abilities and character and potential to impact. Fearing God means reverencing Him for who He is and giving Him the respect that He is due.

When we fear the Lord, we understand a bit of God's power, might, and holiness; God's ability to bless or to destroy, to lift up or take down. We also recognize that God disciplines His children in order to correct their behavior (Psalms 6:1; Hebrews 12:6).

This fear leads to obedience and results in blessing, which the midwives surely know well from the stories of Abraham, who, though waiting years for his promised son, obeyed God when He said, "Take now your son, your only son Isaac, whom you love, and . . . offer him there as a burnt offering" (Genesis 22:2). The midwives know their history, and God's response to Abraham's obedience: "Now I know that you fear God, because you have not withheld from me your son, your only son" (Genesis 22:12 NIV). Oh, if only we knew the stories of faith like these Hebrew women undoubtedly do! These stories of another's footsteps of faith give us the courage to trust and to follow obediently when God calls.

What about their answer to Pharaoh's demand, "Why didn't you kill the babies?" The women's response isn't exactly true. Do the Hebrew women really give birth before the midwives reach them? Possibly, with such a death warrant hanging over newborn heads, the laboring mothers deliberately don't call the midwives for the birthing process. Either way, the midwives know that their ultimate obedience has to be to their unseen King, not to the obsessed ruler of their host country. Because they love God, they act uprightly. Whenever you are faced with two conflicting options, like the midwives, you have to make the decision of which choice will bring God the greatest glory. Because we love God, we too do the right thing. Benefits come from obedience and consequences from disobedience.

Fear of the Lord leads to obedience and results in a whole raft of blessings.

God blesses the midwives by establishing them in households, and their obedience results in the birth of the future deliverer of their people. In fact, the Scriptures tell us that, "By faith [Moses] forsook Egypt, not fearing the wrath of the king; for he endured as seeing Him who is invisible" (Hebrews 11:27). Shiphrah and Puah's courageous example no doubt had an impact on Moses. He would know the stories of the midwives whose tapestry of honor protected his very life.

Though raising eight children, often single-handedly and with few resources, my mother did what was right. She refused to moan about our circumstances, or my father's long days and weeks away with work. She held the Lord and His principles in high esteem. She feared, respected, honored Him, and wanted to bring Him glory. She wanted to showcase the Lord Jesus Christ in her life. And she wanted to pass on a legacy to the generations to come.

The Scriptures tell us in Psalm 112:1, "Blessed is the man who fears the Lord, Who delights greatly in His commandments." Fearing the Lord results in a whole raft of blessings (112:2–8):

> His descendants will be mighty on earth;
> The generation of the upright will be blessed.
> Wealth and riches will be in his house,
> And his righteousness endures forever.
> Unto the upright there arises light in the darkness;
> He is gracious, and full of compassion, and righteous.
> A good man deals graciously and lends;
> He will guide his affairs with discretion.
> Surely he will never be shaken;
> The righteous will be in everlasting remembrance.
> He will not be afraid of evil tidings;
> His heart is steadfast, trusting in the Lord.
> His heart is established;
> He will not be afraid.

Fear of the Lord replaces all other fear, and places us in line with God's plans for our lives. It connects us with the One who promised to bless and establish us when we keep our hearts set on Him.

Midwives for Our Future

We need a Shiphrah and a Puah in our lives. They demonstrate the outworking of the fear of the Lord. We need companions who will help birth in us the dreams God dreams for us. People who will hear the melodies in our hearts and help us to learn to sing them. People who will encourage us toward obedience, even when there seem to be easier roads to travel. Otherwise, we will be enslaved by our fears.

When I (Jane) started writing, I trembled to admit to anyone my attempts to put words on paper. No way would I tell them that one day I hoped to get published. When my small group discerned my secret dream, they poured words of encouragement over me. "You will be a woman of letters one day, Jane," said Marge. Those women became midwives, coaching me not in the process of writing but in the dreaming and then doing. They asked how it was going, celebrated when my first anecdote sold for $25 in a major women's magazine, stayed awake through dreadful first drafts, and valiantly kept from roaring with laughter over their pathetic quality.

My friend Deborah's "midwife" helped her through the struggles of her marriage. She couldn't leave and she couldn't stay, but with her friend's help, she began to focus on her own problems and issues rather than whine about her husband's. Her friend encouraged her to get counseling, to move forward with healing. Was this a road out, an exodus for her? Yes—she moved out of her victim mentality and began to change. And as she changed, her marriage changed. She learned to set boundaries, learned to speak respectfully to her husband, building him up. And as she changed, her husband changed. He marveled at the differences in her: her appearance and her demeanor improved, and he began to fall in love with her again. It was a long, slow delivery, and one that Deborah wouldn't have attempted without her friend.

Who are your midwives? Who will attend you on the birthstool; who will coach you as you move toward the Jordan? Who will step into the river with you and share the miracle of the parting of the waters?

Miracles, like sunsets, are much more powerful when experienced with another. As we were taught as children, use the buddy system. Don't wade into the water alone.

ᏒEfuting the Death Warrant

Shiphrah and Puah, these glistening and glittery women, take hope, clinging to the Author of life, and disregard the king's dictate of death.

Who dictates death for you? Death of hope, death of dreams, death of healing? Your circumstances may be dark. Watch the birth of a day, the rise of light and the demise of night, and refute the death warrant. God is the Author of life, and in His light we see light. New life. Wriggling, bawling, cooing, suckling life, like Puah and Shiphrah witnessed.

The birth is hard but the longing is huge. Ask God to help you long again. Invite God to take you back to the River Jordan, back to the issues, the problems, and the unhealthy fears that separate you from the Promised Land. And remember. Remember where He parted the Red Sea.

Ask Him to do it again. To part the floodwaters of fear in your heart and let you cross over.

Travel Mercies

1. What people in your life glisten and glitter as a result of their relationship with God? Who has heightened your reverence of God, and challenged you to live in obedience to Him? Where have you seen flourishing, even in hardship, as a result of your fear of the Lord? Who acts as a midwife for you, coaching you through the difficulties of life here on earth? Who has helped guide you in the birth of your dreams?

2. What fear roots you to the bank on the wrong side of the River Jordan? What unhealthy fears dominate your heart and work out into your life? In your past, who has dictated death for you? Where have your hopes been crushed? Your heart bruised, your dreams damaged?

3. How can you create safety in your home, even if the world outside sends you into "full fear" mode? In what ways can you make your home a sanctuary?

4. What can you call to mind, and therefore have hope (Lamentations 3:21)? What truth about God? Where have you experienced His hand in the past? Hold on to that memory stone and invite God to work in your heart.

What Mean These Stones?

What stories will you share about fearing the Lord with those around you? Your friends, neighbors, coworkers, children, or grandchildren? Pick one story, and consider how you will tell it. Ask God for the right words and for open hearts of the hearers, that they too might turn their hearts to Him.

Power Up

> Charm is deceitful and beauty is passing,
> But a woman who fears the Lord, she shall be praised.
> Give her of the fruit of her hands,
> And let her own works praise her in the gates.
> —Proverbs 31:30-31

Rock-Hard Truth

"We must be willing to promote the program of God rather than yield to the pressure of the culture."
—Lois Evans

Remember Me, O Lord

Heavenly Father,
We remember Your promise
to bring Your children into a land of their own.
And we remember You called us, as well, with a holy calling.
Help us to focus on You, on Your calling in our lives.

Attend us on the birthstool of our dreams and desires,
and deliver us from our pain and our fear.
Do not allow us to succumb to the death warrant of this world,
but to cling to Your plans for our lives.
Amen.

Memory Stone

The works of the Lord are great,
Studied by all who have pleasure in them.
His work is honorable and glorious,
And His righteousness endures forever.
He has made His wonderful works to be remembered;
The Lord is gracious and full of compassion.

— *Psalm 111:2–4*

CHAPTER THREE

JOCHEBED:

REMEMBERING THE COMPASSION OF GOD

Her mother's and father's deep love for her gave Shirley a foundation for understanding God's love. As a bony kneed teenager, Shirley always rode her bike to youth group at church, and one day, an evangelist declared that anyone born into the family of God through a relationship with Jesus Christ was royalty. She invited this Christ into her heart, and knew for the first time the depth of a love that her parents' love merely shadowed. Her parents made her feel like a princess; Christ declared her a child of the King!

This internal sense of royalty, of God glorying in her, fortified Shirley in the hard times in the South, times of poverty in a sharecropper's family, then of working alongside her husband building a struggling family business into a booming distribution center. And when her husband served her divorce papers thirty years into their marriage, it was God's love and compassion for her that stiffened her *backbone and enabled her to step regally into her Jordan River.*

Knowing her position in the royal family of God allowed her to overcome the stigma of divorce and the loneliness of singlehood as grandmother and mother. Because God gloried in her, Shirley did her grief work faithfully, and gradually quit pining for her husband. She refused to allow bitterness to corrode her heart. Today, hope and love radiate from her. Because she remembers God's compassion, His amazing love.

A Compassionate Woman

Like Shirley, Moses' mother learns early in life of God's glorious love and compassion. Born into the tribe of Levi, her people would be appointed by God to stand in the gap for the Hebrews, between God and earthly rulers; they would seek God's face and reflect God's glory—His love, His holiness, His compassion, His justice—to others. Moses, the son of this Levite woman, would one day speak with God and be His mouthpiece to the Hebrew people, his face literally glowing with the glory of God (see Exodus 34:29–35).

Proverbs 22:1 tells us, "A good name is to be chosen rather than great riches, loving favor rather than silver or gold." Does King Solomon have Moses' mother in mind when he pens that proverb? Exodus 6:20 and Numbers 26:59 record her name: Jochebed. *Jehovah gloried.* "Heavy with glory." Her parents surely give her a name to live up to. Is there a richer name for a woman in all of Scripture? And truly, Jochebed's life plays out as a woman who knows she is loved, knows that God gloried when He created her. She surely brings that glowing compassion and love with her to her marriage, her parenting, her position in society. She knows God's love; it must inform all her actions, allowing her to do the unthinkable. She remembers, calling that love to mind when her son, her son with a death warrant hanging over his tiny head, is ushered into the world by Shiphrah's and Puah's sure hands.

ℒiving in Captivity

As a Hebrew in Egypt, Jochebed is born into captivity, like her parents before her, like her children after her. What happens to people who live in captivity? Captors hope their prisoners become cowed by authority, unable to think for themselves, unwilling to risk their lives for the principle of good. That they lose their spirit and spunk. That they become exactly what their captors want them to be: submissive, blind, fearful.

More recent history demonstrates this as well. The aim of World War II concentration camps was, as Terrence Des Pres wrote:

> . . . to reduce inmates to mindless creatures whose behavior could be predicted and controlled absolutely. The camps have so far been the closest thing on earth to a perfect Skinner Box. They were a closed, completely regulated environment, a "total" world in the strict sense. Pain and death were the "negative reinforcers," food and life the "positive reinforcers," and all these forces were pulling and shoving twenty-four hours a day at the deepest stratum of human need.[4]

But that experiment failed, as did Pharaoh's forced slavery of the Israelites. The captors did not figure on God's presence in those places of captivity. Philip Yancey says, "Within the malnourished bodies of the inmates there is a highly developed sense of *morality*, *art*, and *hope*. None of those qualities is to be expected in such a place. Yet they spring up like fountains out of granite."[5]

Like a geyser in the desert, another possibility exists; and like those prisoners during World War II, Jochebed demonstrates it with her life. She becomes captivating while in captivity in Egypt.

How do we live well in such situations? Whether captivity looks like a grunt-work job or a difficult marriage, a prodigal child or single parenting, illness or a prison sentence, our River Jordan presents us with a choice about how to behave and who to become in those places. What will spring forth from our captivity?

I certainly remember feeling captive during heavy child-rearing years, with Tony working long hours. As women, we have to be aware of our feelings so that we don't take them out on others. When

I finally opened up to my husband about my overwhelmed heart, we arranged a system. I greeted him at the door when he returned from work, and we kissed on my way out to the mall. I had to get away, whether I bought anything or not. I also chose to leave some of the disciplinary responsibility to Tony so that we were equals in the home and I didn't feel like the great burden bearer.

At other times, the demands in the church were too big for my developmental stage. I learned delegation because I didn't possess those gifts. In your life too, whether you are feeling pulled by your job, ministry, husband, or children, you must learn to delegate without shame or embarrassment the areas that aren't part of your package of gifts. Otherwise, the work of your hands could feel like slavery.

Maybe you feel held hostage by your family situation: no parents offer emotional support, no husband helps raise the children and run the home. Don't let Satan trap you into being a captive! Don't let the Enemy trick you into harming yourself or someone else. If no one is there to help, find a surrogate mother for your motherless heart, or a good friend to share your frustrations with. It takes the body of Christ to raise a family; make use of the one God has given you in your local church.

Jochebed refuses to capitulate under the rock-hard cultural pressures of Egypt and slavery. She has other options: Jochebed could just kill her son. She could have an abortion. After all, Pharaoh approves murdering babies, the norm in the culture. But she fears God more than man. She commits to God's plan and program in spite of what the culture considered normal and permissible.

Jochebed embodies the words the Lord would speak many years later to Israel, living in exile in yet another foreign country, under yet another foreign power:

> Build houses and dwell in them; plant gardens and eat their fruit.
> Take wives and beget sons and daughters; and take wives for your
> sons and give your daughters to husbands, so that they may bear
> sons and daughters—that you may be increased there, and not
> diminished. And seek the peace of the city where I have caused
> you to be carried away captive, and pray to the Lord for it; for in
> its peace you will have peace (Jeremiah 29:5–7).

How comforting to know that if we live in captivity, it is sometimes because God has allowed us to be carried there. And that in our places of captivity, He wants us to choose to live well there, to build homes and to raise godly families, and to pray for our captors. His desire is for us to flourish, to increase, not to be diminished.

Joy lived like this for years. When her husband lost his job, no one could guess that his unemployment would last eighteen months, forcing them to subsist on her substitute teacher's income. But even with the strong probability that they would lose their home, Joy refused to live as a slave to fear, anger, resentment. Like Jochebed, she did not capitulate. Her demeanor of trust and peace glorified God and testified to His faithfulness. Whether that faithfulness looked like a case of canned corn, an anonymous bag of groceries, or a money order in the mail, God did not abandon them in their captivity, and they did not abandon their hearts or their faith there either. Even in the dark they knew God's compassion and continued to seek Him to light the way.

The Lord's further promise to the Israelites and to us in our places of captivity is this:

> For thus says the Lord: After seventy years are completed at Babylon, I will visit you and perform My good word toward you, and cause you to return to this place. For I know the thoughts that I think toward you, says the Lord, thoughts of peace and not of evil, to give you a future and a hope. Then you will call upon Me and go and pray to Me, and I will listen to you. And you will seek Me and find Me, when you search for Me with all your heart. I will be found by you, says the Lord, and I will bring you back from your captivity (Jeremiah 29:10–14).

The Israelites refuse to succumb to the slave mentality. They choose to live regally, royally, as God's chosen people, and to continue to embrace the God who directs their paths. Though that path includes captivity, they remember His promise to Abraham and cling to the promise of their own land, a promise born out of God's compassion for His people. Like the queen of England who took her daughter to a royal function, only to see her slumping in her chair.

After several reminders to "Sit up straight, please!" the queen finally said, "Don't you know who you are? You're a child of the king."

$\mathcal{A}$ Captivating Woman

Part of Jochebed's beauty is her evident strength of faith and of character as a wife, as there is little mention of the role Amram plays in their marriage or in raising their children. Perhaps Amram is busy about his work, leaving Jochebed to head the family by default, a lonely wife left alone in their Egyptian home. Perhaps she functions as a single mother in many ways; this would not be unusual in that society.

God strengthens us to mirror His compassion, lively interest, confidence, and loving-kindness.

A strong and capable woman is a gift to her children's development. Jochebed does not use her aloneness as an excuse for poor parenting; she refuses to excuse herself from the role God miraculously gives her. Apparently, she invests deeply in the lives of her children, and undoubtedly lives up to her name, "Jehovah gloried." His love and compassion surely show as she raises her children, teaching them about Him while they slave through their days. She must mirror for Aaron, Miriam, and Moses the compassion of God, the lively interest, confidence, and loving-kindness of the God of Israel.

Like Jochebed, we become the mirror for our husband, our children, or the people we influence. And like Jochebed, though married, maybe there is little presence of your husband in your home. You may feel like a single parent. Maybe you are married to a passive man, who has relinquished the leadership role, isn't acting like the spiritual head of the home, or who feels inadequate in light of your gifts. Perhaps your children's knowledge of Scripture intimidates him; many husbands have said to us, "My kids know more than I do." Some women are more well-versed in Scripture, and the husband might feel inadequate, not just in this specific area, but in other areas as well.

"How can I get my husband to be a better leader in our home?" women ask frequently: married women living with passive men, or with men who are working on their leadership skills because they weren't brought up in an environment with this training as part of the mix. "How do I respect his position as I execute what we have agreed on?" It takes a rock-hard faith and commitment to live in that place. If your helpmate doesn't seem to be much help, if he isn't taking the lead, "How," as my husband says, "can you follow a parked car?"

LIVING WITH A NON-LEADER
1. Pray for him.
2. Find accountability friends to ensure you are a godly wife and woman.
3. Invite him into relationship with you through love and acceptance.

Pray for him. C. H. Spurgeon said, "One night alone in prayer might make us new men, changed from poverty of soul to spiritual wealth, from trembling to triumphing."[6] I cannot count the women who committed themselves to pray and fast for their husbands, and in the process of praying for their men, the women were changed! They became more godly, beautiful women, and their beauty and the power of God worked on their husbands' hearts. Frequently, their men became the men, the husbands, and daddies they were called to be.

When a man fails to lead in the home, whether from lack of training or lack of desire, his wife needs to respectfully, then discreetly, take the lead with the attitude of helping. Many women are more gifted, skilled, and talented than their mates in some areas. We can't expect our husbands to have the same gifting and passion as we do. As women of the Word, we still need to be all that we were created to be and do, but following God's way, because we are guaranteed that if we do it God's way we will be blessed.

Call out the best in your husband; speak to his good characteristics. Admire those traits aloud. Assume the best about him, rather than the worst. And when he is passive, ask kind and thoughtful questions: "What do you think about Timmy's problem at school? Do you think he should say such-and-such to the child on the playground?" "What do you think about our budget? Does this seem to be allocated correctly? What is missing?"

Walk through the doors
that are open and stop pounding
on the doors that are closed.

Learn to ask more leading questions. Rather than whining, "You never take me on a date," suggest instead, "This movie we've been talking about seeing is showing now. Would Friday be a good night to see it?" You may have had to initiate it, but, ladies, that's still a date.

Or, what if you and your husband have agreed to share family devotions on a certain evening, and the husband initially responds positively, but then lacks consistency or falls off? For the mother who wants Deuteronomy 6 to be real in her children's lives, ask, "Do you think this is a good time for devotions, before the kids go to sleep?" or "Is tonight the night for our devotions?" If her husband does not pick up the baton, at least she has given him the respect of leading, and then the wife chooses to carry out the responsibility on his behalf.

Give him the chance to shine in his strengths by involving him in leadership. Where is your husband gifted? Invite him to use those gifts at home. Walk through the doors that are open and stop pounding on the doors that are closed. Focus on what is working in your marriage. And if your husband is an unbeliever, your actions will speak much more loudly than your words. He will see your respect and love by the way you live in your home and the way you treat him, and you will win your husband "without a word" (1 Peter 3:1).

Leading takes practice, and almost always involves failure first. When he leads, even if he leads poorly, thank him for leading. Don't try to tell him where he messed up; rather, praise him for his presence. And pass the baton to him again and again. If women are always honking their discontent like geese complaining about the cold, then husbands will never take the lead. The thermostat in the home will keep going down until it is frigid.

$\mathcal{A}$ Perceptive Woman

God's glory shines through a woman when she sees life with His eyes of compassion. Even in captivity, our eyes can be open to the glory of God in another, giving us hearts filled with grace. The Scriptures tell us that when Jochebed saw that Moses "was a beautiful child, she hid him three months" (Exodus 2:2). The book of Hebrews reports that she and Amram recognized Moses as "no ordinary child" (Hebrews 11:23 NIV), and so they protected his life, refusing to comply with the king's orders to drown their boy babies in the Nile.

Psalm 127:3–5 reads,

> Behold, children are a heritage from the Lord,
> The fruit of the womb is a reward.
> Like arrows in the hand of a warrior,
> So are the children of one's youth.
> Happy is the man who has his quiver full of them.

And truly, no one is ordinary in God's eyes. God remembers that we are but dust, and has compassion on us. His view of us shapes His love for us. This helps me when I run into people who seem riddled with dysfunction. Jane says, "Wounded people wound others." As we learn to look at people as a product of their past, not excusing their past but rather understanding their present, we see them with God's eyes, see them as someone God glories in as well.

God's love for us shapes His view of us.

And when we see others as extraordinary in God's eyes, as beautiful, fine, "no ordinary child," then we too will protect their lives. Like Jochebed, we will hide them in our love and invite them into a life that is hid in Christ's. We will remember aloud with them the glory and goodness of God's love and action in our lives, and then they too will begin to reflect that same glory, to recognize that God glories in them because we love them with God's love.

Perhaps when you were a child no one looked on you with a heart transformed by the love of God; no one saw you as beautiful or fine. You do not have to live with others' wrong assessments of you any longer. The God of the universe glories in you! You can be free from the captivity of others' treatment of you, and learn to walk as royalty.

A Wise Woman

Jochebed invests in her family, raising a generation of leaders, courageous people who will stand in the gap, defy rulers and principalities for the one true God and the salvation of His people. They will risk their lives and reputations for the glory of God.

This woman in whom Jehovah glories sends her daughter to track the progress of her baby brother down the Nile. Do they role-play before the baby's float trip? "Now, if someone finds the baby, what will you do?" or "If the basket overturns, how will you handle it?" However she preps Miriam for her vigil along the Nile, her daughter is well equipped for the task.

A Compassionate Woman

Nursing mothers have a built-in baby barometer: if there is no means of expressing the milk, the pain becomes intense and nearly unbearable. I wonder about that as Jochebed watches from the riverbank as her son floats off, his contentment turning to cries of distress. The physical pain alone would make it difficult to let a baby float away to the dangerous unknowns of the Niles in this world. But combine that with the emotional wrenching and the aching arms of not holding the baby, and the image of Jochebed at the riverbank becomes one of deep grief. An image that we can relate to as women, forced to let go of dreams, hopes, and loved ones.

It would be impossible for Jochebed to forget her baby. Her body and her heart will not allow it. So it is with God. His hands and heart will not allow forgetfulness. The Lord tells us, in Isaiah 49:15–16,

> Can a woman forget her nursing child,
> And not have compassion on the son of her womb?
> Surely they may forget,
> Yet I will not forget you.
> See, I have inscribed you on the palms of My hands.

This woman must know God's compassion intimately, and trusts Him with the life of her child. She remembers God's care of her, His calling of her, and clings to that warm, sweet memory even as her warm, sweet baby floats downstream. She knows that God will not forget her, nor can He possibly forget her son.

Jochebed does not know the fate awaiting her infant boy, only that the God of all compassion and Father of all mercy goes before him. No doubt she plants herself at the water's edge, her heart swelling into her throat, her prayers leading him away. She surely stands in the gap for the child-man who will stand in the gap between God and man. She releases her grip on the edge of the basket. She lets go of her son.

Imagine her joy when Miriam runs, gasping, calling her name, "Mama! Mama! Come with me!" And clutching her mother's hand, Miriam tears back down the riverbank, pulling to a stop when finally reaching Pharaoh's daughter. The princess is hiring Jochebed to nurse the very child of her womb.

This mother trusts God so much that she lets her baby go—and receives him back, nursing him through his diaper days, telling him stories of his people, rocking him and singing over him, loving him, giving him a solid foundation. Not only physically through nursing, but spiritually, as she remembers story after story aloud with him, teaching him on her lap, at her knee, as they walked and as they worked.

He learns of his people, of his God, the God of Abraham, Isaac, and Jacob. Remembering God's compassion prepares a mother to let go of her son.

And prepares a son to convince a pharaoh to "Let my people go."

Jehovah Glories

Jehovah gloried when He created Jochebed, and He gloried when creating you. Regardless of what your parents named you, regardless of how they raised you, regardless of how they showed their love for you, God gloried when creating you. Perhaps you didn't know that kind of love as a child. Perhaps your life has been mottled with fear instead of wrapped in compassion. Maybe you have never known how it feels to be gloried in, to know an unforgettable, unforgetting, never-let-go kind of love from another. The people in our lives will inevitably forget or fail to love us well. They will bungle their attempts at intimacy. They may totally abandon us.

If we look to anyone except God
for a never-let-go kind of love,
we look in the wrong place.

The dreamboat of a man will turn out to be fallible. Our children will be imperfect and will disappoint us. Our parents will leave scars on us, because they were scarred by their parents and by life in a world that dictates death. Perhaps your children didn't turn out the way you'd hoped, or they have abandoned you or their faith as they got on with their own lives. It is impossible to avoid brokenness and failure in relationships.

If we look to anyone except God for a never-let-go kind of love, then we look in the wrong place, and we ask for disappointment. God Himself has promised to never leave us or forsake us (Hebrews 13:5), and to never forget us.

He has carved your name into the palm of His hand. This Jehovah, the same Jehovah who gloried when creating Jochebed, glories now as He loves you.

Step into the River

What is your River Jordan? What keeps you from crossing over? Sometimes it is blame: blaming everyone else for not taking that first step; blaming your parents for their dysfunction or total absence; blaming a boss, or a husband who doesn't lead, or anyone who might absorb the blame and the accompanying shame, so that you can continue to make excuses and stay on the wrong side of the river. Blaming your absentee father or your broken or unavailable mother, or blaming your husband or your lack of a husband, or your children or lack of children, or your employment or unemployment, or the hardships you've experienced on this side of the Jordan.

If we choose to blame,
we forfeit the game.
And the Enemy wins.

This Enemy does not want you to cross over. He wants you to stand, wistfully, on the desert side of the Jordan. He wants blame to incapacitate you, to decapitate you, to keep you from looking to our true Head, Jesus, and setting forth in the waters of the River Jordan.

Our parents' name for us, their raising of us, changes nothing about the truth: that God gloried in us from before our conception ("Before you were in the womb, I knew you") and glories in us now.

Remembering, knowing that kind of love, changes our lives. It enables us to impact others with the same kind of loving attention and compassion that Jochebed demonstrated.

It is time to let go.
And step into the Jordan River.

Travel Mercies

1. What is your captivity? What choices have you made in captivity? How hard is it to trust God's promise of a future and a hope? To pray for your captors, whether past or present, and to refuse bitterness and corrosion of spirit?

2. Who gloried in you as a child? Who failed to love you well? What wounds do you carry, what scars on your spirit, that hinder you from letting God glory in you?

3. If you are married, what are your disappointments there? Where do you hope for the leader to emerge in your husband? How do you deal with any failures you might see in him, as a husband, a father, a provider, a friend, a lover? And if you are not married, what are your disappointments, sorrows, woundings there?

4. Where does blame fit into your coping system for daily life? How has it incapacitated you? Where does it show up in your primary relationships: your marriage, your parenting, your friendships, your dating life?

5. What do you need to let go of? What would it look like to let go?

What Mean These Stones?

When have you experienced God's never-let-go love? Try to frame that story, those stories, in such a way that you can share them with others. As you remember God's compassionate love, you will be encouraged to share those stories with others.

Power Up

*"Before I formed you in the womb I knew you;
Before you were born I sanctified you;
I ordained you a prophet to the nations."*
—Jeremiah 1:5

Rock-Hard Truth

"Letting go takes all the energy I have."[7]
—Jennifer Kennedy Dean

Remember Me, O Lord

*Heavenly Father,
who glories in me,
thank You.
Thank You for carving my name
into the palms of Your hands;
Thank You for loving me
with the only never-let-go love that exists.
Help me to know that love,
to heal from the wounds of others' imperfect love.
And help me to love others as well,
to glory in Your presence within them.
In Jesus' name,
who still bears our scars,
Amen.*

Memory Stone

He has put a new song in my mouth—
Praise to our God;
Many will see it and fear,
And will trust in the Lord.

— *Psalm 40:3*

CHAPTER FOUR

MIRIAM:

REMEMBERING THE SONG OF GOD

Melinda was in her home office on September 11, 2001. Though far from the disaster, her heart broke as she watched television footage, listened to the radio when in her car, and kept tuned in to the story's tragic unfolding. Throughout her vigil, she wept before God for the victims, for the destruction, for the horror. "Where were You, God?" she asked over and over.

In answer, a hymn emerged from the recesses of her soul, hidden there for years:

"How firm a foundation, ye saints of the Lord,
    is laid for your faith in His excellent word!
What more can He say than to you He hath said,
    to you who for refuge to Jesus have fled?
Fear not, I am with thee, O be not dismayed,
    for I am thy God and will still give thee aid;

*I'll strengthen and help thee and cause thee to stand
upheld by My righteous, omnipotent hand."*

*Melinda typed out all the verses, laminated them,
and clutched them in her pocket. When her heart grew
troubled, she remembered God's promises, pulled out the
song, and began to sing. The song of faith carried her
through the weeks and months of anxiety as she remembered God's might and power and goodness.*

ℳiriam's Story

In *The Prince of Egypt*, the bright, willow-wisp child weaves through the brush alongside the Nile, keeping her brother's floating cradle in sight, following his treacherous path downriver. She gasps as alligators snap powerful jaws at the boat. She holds her breath as the infant's journey includes rocks and rapids and waves. And she sighs in relief when the basket washes to the shoreline where the princess bathes, surrounded by her helpers.

When Moses is drawn from the Nile, crying but safe at last, the girl hidden in the bushes emerges, all wide-eyed innocence. With daring cleverness, she asks, "Shall I go and get one of the Hebrew women to nurse the baby for you?" (Exodus 2:7 NIV).

Miriam's leadership skills appear at a young age. How possessive she must be of her little brother; how proud to be the one to watch his progress down the Nile and then to watch his progress at their mother's breast when Pharaoh's daughter pays Jochebed to nurse Moses. What a loss to give him up once again after he is weaned, when he is tutored in the king's courts.

𝒲atching the Leader

Miriam plays a significant part in preserving the infant life of the one who would lead Israel to freedom. But how does she feel, watching and waiting all those years, while he is raised in splendor in Pharaoh's courts? Impatient, frustrated? Does she glimpse the role Moses would perform, in light of God's dramatic intercession in his life?

Then, at age forty, Moses intervenes in a fight between an Egyptian supervisor and a Hebrew slave. Killing the Egyptian, he buries him in the sand (see Exodus 2:11–12). How does Miriam react, seeing her brother, her beloved, chosen brother, rescued from the Nile and given such a divine preparation for leadership—tutored in Pharaoh's court!—running for his life because he is now a murderer? Surely she is angry with her hotheaded, impetuous sibling.

Converting Anger

How easy it would be to hold on to such an anger. How easy to meditate on another's actions, and how they impacted you, harmed you, changed your life, delayed your plans, ruined your timetable. How do you release such contaminating anger, however justified it might be?

Or maybe you are the one running for your life. You have hurt others and run to get away from the consequences. Or you have been so severely wounded that anger has been your armor, protecting your heart and soul from further damage.

Holding on to the anger, or running from the consequences of anger, is sin. It will destroy you.

The protective covering can become the chink in your armor: a hardened heart can kill you.

Get rid of the anger. Anger isn't wrong: it is an honest reaction to life in a broken, unjust world. "Be angry," says the Lord, "and do not sin" (Ephesians 4:26). Holding on to the anger, or running from the consequences of anger, is sin. It will destroy you.

Own your anger by recognizing it and how it shows up in your life. Take note of the ways your anger has hurt you and others. Then bring it before God. "Oh, Lord. I am angry at _____ for hurting me." Or, "Dear God, I am angry about _____." Confess how you have sinned in your anger, and ask the Lord, who promises to forgive us our sins and cleanse us from all unrighteousness (1 John 1:9), to restore you to wholeness, to take away the anger and replace it with forgiveness for the one who has hurt or disappointed you.

Many years after the exodus, the Lord tells the Israelites, "I sent Moses to lead you, also Aaron and Miriam" (Micah 6:4 NIV). Miriam cannot lead her people alongside her brothers if she harbors anger in her heart. Neither can we, as women called to lead others in official and unofficial ways, allow anger to take root and begin its slow strangulation of heart and soul. God has called us to freedom!

ℒetting Go . . . Again

Quite a transition must occur when Moses returns from Midian, after forty years of wilderness sheep watching. He gathers Aaron and Miriam to begin the process of leading the Israelites out of Egypt. Protective Miriam needs to learn to come alongside Moses but not rescue him; to co-lead with her brothers rather than play mini-mother to them.

Immediately they run into public contempt. When Moses demands his people's release before Pharaoh, the Egyptians tighten the screws on their slaves, imposing impossible standards. OSHA would not have been pleased! The Hebrews scorn Moses and Aaron for going before Pharaoh: "Let the Lord look on you and judge, because you have made us abhorrent in the sight of Pharaoh and in the sight of his servants, to put a sword in their hand to kill us" (Exodus 5:21).

How does Miriam detach from reputation and resist the temptation to fix and people-please? How does she stand firm alongside Moses and Aaron, withstand public disfavor, and hold fast to God's plan for the Israelites?

Miriam has seen God's hand. She saw Him protect Moses in his tiny ark on the waters of the Nile; she saw Him direct a princess to the banks at just the right time to rescue her brother. She saw the unfolding miracle. Miriam knows that God intervenes in lives, knows that God has a purpose for His chosen ones. So when it is time to rally God's people and route them into the desert, she is ready. She can easily call to mind the Lord's intervention in her own life, and thus call her people to walk by faith.

Remembering God's hand on our lives, God's saving and calling and sending forth, gives us the courage to let go of our need to protect ourself, our reputation, our loved ones. Only God can deliver us. Remembering God's hold on us enables us to let go, so God can let His people go.

When we let our people go, relinquishing our need to direct and protect people and releasing them to God, then we are free to be the women He invites us to be. Letting go frees us to sing the unique song the Lord gives each of us.

Victory Songs

When Moses, Miriam, and Aaron lead the Hebrew people out of Egypt, when the wheels snap off the Egyptians' chariots, when the people turn and see the Red Sea crashing over their enemies, Moses breaks out in a victory song. Exodus 15:20–21 tells us that, in response, "Miriam the prophetess, the sister of Aaron, took the timbrel in her hand; and all the women went out after her with timbrels and with dances. And Miriam answered them:

> 'Sing to the Lord,
> For He has triumphed gloriously!
> The horse and its rider
> He has thrown into the sea!' "

They sing; they dance; they praise the wonderful acts of God. The people commit to memory the triumphant work of God. Moses' song extols the character and the deeds of God as He delivers the Israelites

from slavery into victory and freedom. It is the first song recorded in
Scripture, and Miriam is the first female leader and prophetess.

*Do you run from remembering your
past, or do you seek to find God there?*

The Israelites' song is a song of remembrance. But perhaps your
memories are not exalted places where God showed up, places of
great victory and triumphant conquering of enemies. Perhaps the
song you would write is a song of pain, of poverty, of brokenness or
disappointment. Perhaps you have no song left to sing; the notes are
snuffed out like a candle in the wind.

Do you run, then, from the memories? Or do you seek to find
God there, in the past, and invite Him to show you how to find Him?
When Jenna first began remembering, all she could see was the lack
of a father in her life. He had disappeared when she was two months
old, and her song was one of abandonment. It is important to sing the
song as the words appear.

But she did not give up. She invited God to show her where He
had been all her life, and the verses to her song began to emerge. He
had provided her with surrogate fathers throughout her journey:
good, kind, caring men who demonstrated heavenly care in an earthly,
broken place. The neighbor who fixed her bike, the youth leader
who listened to her pain, the teacher who patiently showed her the
secrets to geometry, the college professor who helped her understand her gifts, the pastor and family who adopted her during an in-
ternship, the married friend who loved his wife in such a way that she
could see how a marriage based on God's love looked.

And Jenna's song, her victory song, ultimately extolled a God
who had fathered her through His people on earth, not allowing her
to remain trapped with an orphan's heart and a story of abandonment. A Father who loved her and watched over her, protected and
provided for her.

Sometimes, though, we forget the words to our song. Sometimes, in spite of a history of God's presence and power—in spite of freedom—we refuse to remember and instead forge ahead on our own, floundering on the freedom.

$\mathcal{D}$esert Failure

The people are waiting for Moses to return. God has called Moses to a summit meeting atop Mount Sinai. The Hebrews stare anxiously at the mountain, then at one another. They watch the cloud, waiting. Waiting. Waiting for God, waiting for Moses, waiting for the desert to end and the dessert of the Promised Land to begin. Where is he? Forty days and forty nights of waiting. In their waiting, they pressure Aaron. "Come, make for us a god who will go before us; as for this Moses, the man who brought us up from the land of Egypt, we do not know what has become of him" (Exodus 32:1 NASB).

In the midst of the peer pressure, do Aaron's leadership and authority go to his head? He puts out a call for jewelry, melts it down and fashions it into a calf, then invites the Israelites to offer sacrifices to their new god.

What of Miriam? She is ominously absent from the scriptural records. Where is Aaron's colleague and sister? Where is the woman of faith, the woman who shook tambourines and sang songs of liberation? Why didn't the co-leader lead, challenging her brother to keep the faith and hold fast to what they both knew to be true: that God is faithful, that He will always deliver His people and keep His promises? Has Miriam let go too much?

Waiting can convert passion to passivity. Waiting can give us memory-blank: we wonder where is God and what is taking so long? Waiting can lead us astray and into forgetfulness—forgetting our calling, our driving passion, forgetting who God is and how He has been faithful.

Miriam's silence speaks loudly. As a woman, whether married or not, you have the ability and the position to speak into situations, to call forth truth, and to remind others of what they seem to be forgetting. You can do this without manipulation, without demanding your own way, without shaming the other. Perhaps it doesn't change the outcome of the situation, but sometimes people are waiting for a word of faith to remind them to hold true, to remember the one true God, to remember His promises, and to cling to what they know but are not experiencing.

Many times I (Jane) have regretted remaining silent and opinion-less when my husband had a hard decision to make. I have sorrowed over my passivity with my children, or in the neighborhood, or in the world, when I have not spoken the word of faith in a pressing situation. Why the silence? Partly because I haven't been still enough along the way, still enough to listen to God and to listen to my own heart, and thus am wordless when it comes to speaking a word of faith to another. And partly I remain silent because I doubt that I have anything of worth to say, anything that will contribute to the moment and to the future, which hangs on the current decision. Or I remain silent because I don't want to lose favor in the sight of another, when my words might differ from theirs. Finally, in all honesty, I sometimes remain silent because I don't want to do the right thing, or I want to have the secret satisfaction of gloating over another's fall.

Our silence as women grieves the Lord, who plants His Word and His Spirit within us, coaches us in the night, and longs for us to give voice to His thoughts: to speak hope and love and truth and faith and courage into others' lives.

When we can be still and know and remember that He is God (Psalm 46:10), then we can come fresh from God's heart and speak out of that knowing stillness.

Will it change the world? That is up to God. But it will change us to hold fast to Him and to speak out of that holding place.

Bitter Times

Many months pass before Miriam appears again in Scripture. Where is the Miriam we know, the sister who helped lead the people between the walls of the sea? Miriam's voice next emerges in Numbers 12:1: "Then Miriam and Aaron spoke against Moses." The verb "spoke" is in the feminine singular, meaning that Miriam is the chief complainant and Aaron is in an inactive role. His sister tries to incite rebellion when she demands, "Has the Lord indeed spoken only through Moses? Has He not spoken through us also?" (12:2).

Miriam, it seems, finally lives up to her name, which means bitter or rebellious. Why do her bitterness and her rebellious spirit appear now?

There is nothing like being in a position of leadership to apply pressure to our souls. It is easy to revert to the chains of the past. Miriam was born into bitter times in the history of her people. Her name reflects the bitter bondage in Egypt. Just so, our past can catch us in the present and hinder us from walking into the future with our heads held high.

But we must not judge another's fall. Rather, learn:

Where there is a rupture, look for the wound.

Childhood Wounds

Jochebed, Miriam's mother, surely was a woman of God with an outlandish faith. "Yeah, yeah," you are saying. "Miriam had it going for her. A great mother who delighted in her children; a mom who likely lived a consistent, godly life; who knew that God gloried in her and who translated that for her children. I can't relate to that kind of life."

Exactly. Who can? There is no such thing as a perfect family or a perfect childhood. While her mother's name meant "Jehovah gloried," and we can assume that any mother whose three children turn out to be fabulous leaders in the history of the world must have done something right, we don't know much about how Miriam was actually raised.

Imagine, in fact, the trauma of growing up in a country where the slaughter of innocents occurred daily. Where the threat of extinguishment at the hands of the Egyptians effaced the joy of pregnancy and childbirth. Where the innocence of childhood meant death if your chromosomes were wrong. The corporate grief must have been wretched.

We don't know if Miriam lost brothers to the king's edict. But wouldn't the fear and death permeating the Hebrew settlement impact Miriam's childhood? Fear replaced safety, leaving an acidic taste in the people's mouths and corroding their hearts. It settled over them like a fog. Surely cries rose from the mothers whose sons were murdered; surely the breaking hearts shattered many nights.

This is no childhood. Childhood meant murder, and the little girls grew up too quickly.

*Wounds do not give us
the right to wound others.*

Inevitably, you too were wounded in childhood, wounded as a young woman, wounded as an adult. Perhaps you were forced to grow up too quickly. You parented your siblings or even your own parents, becoming the "little mother" or the responsible one. Your circumstances robbed you of childhood play, of dreaming and dawdling. Perhaps you understood that no place was safe.

When do those wounds appear: now, as an adult? Do they show up as bitterness and grumbling and jealousy, as in Miriam's case? Do you become passive, wanting to force another to lead because you always had to be the leader in the past? Do your wounds show up as manipulation—trying to begin a revolt against another, a golden calf moment—or seep out in anger?

Wounds do not give us the right to wound others. The more quickly we deal with our injured hearts, the more quickly we route the enemies of blame, of sin, of jealousy and bitterness. Cynthia Heald, best-selling author and speaker, says, "Bringing up the past is like drinking poison." If you drink the dregs of bitterness, it will kill you, putting you into a depression; all the while other people are going on with their lives. Deal with it and put it behind you. Then the Enemy of your soul is unable to gag the song of faith that waits to emerge.

*O*utside the Camp

When Miriam's complaint rises from the camp, God acts swiftly, calling the threesome to the tabernacle. He appears in the pillar of cloud, and His words tolerate no argument in response. Miriam dared to question His anointed servant, Moses, and tried to rope Aaron into her sin. God will not allow such manipulation. It would destroy His people.

When God leaves the Tent of Meeting, Miriam's sin appears on her skin: she is white with leprosy.

I love her family's response. They band together, the powerful leaders once again uniting. Immediately Aaron turns to Moses, begging him to intercede before God for their sister. And Moses quickly forgives his sister's bitter spirit and rushes to God's presence, crying, "Please heal her, O God, I pray!" (Numbers 12:13).

God shuts her outside the camp for seven days. And the community of Israelites waits for her, refusing to move on until God restores her to their companionship.

We can't let others' wounding criticism or jealousy separate us from God or from our family in Christ. Like Moses, can you move to forgiveness and then move to God's side, begging Him to forgive the one who has hurt you?

Singing Toward the Future

Somehow, in spite of the wounds of her youth, Miriam learns to sing.

It is hard to sing when death abounds. The notes curdle on the terror and grief in our throats, and yet the commandment "Sing" appears frequently in the Old Testament. Singing, like prayer, routs the Enemy when we sing to the Lord, when we remember His faithfulness, when we hold fast to what we know from experience to be true about Him.

We can apply Joyce Meyer's words to our songs in the night and our songs in the day; we want to be women of the Word and prayer so that when Satan and his demons see my feet hit the floor in the morning, they say, "Oh no! She's up again!"[8] In the words of the spiritual, we're "Gonna sing when the Spirit says 'Sing.'"

So we learn to sing through and around our pain, to remember aloud God's goodness, to put a melody line of praise to the somber notes that fill our lives. The Enemy will not win this round, nor the next, nor the next, because we can stand on the powerful name of Jesus and remember what He has done for us: in a manger, in a garden, on a cross, and an empty tomb. We remember the Red Seas of our life and know that our Deliverer will triumph yet again. We will rout the Enemy by recalling God's goodness and His overarching plan for our life, by calling on Christ's life and death and resurrection as surety for the future. We will refuse the bitterness, the anger, the jealousy, and stand firm.

Philippians 2:9–11 triumphantly states, "Therefore God also has highly exalted Him and given Him the name which is above every name, that at the name of Jesus every knee should bow, of those in heaven, and of those on earth, and of those under the earth, and that every tongue should confess that Jesus Christ is Lord, to the glory of God the Father."

The Enemy cannot stand when you sing out the name of Jesus.

So sing your song. Hum the melody. Lip-sync the words until you can sing them from your heart. It doesn't matter if you can carry a tune or if you sound like you're wearing a bucket over your head. It doesn't matter if you know any notes at all. Your songs of praise create a bridge into your future, a bridge over your River Jordan.

Travel Mercies

1. Where are you protecting others? Yourself? How can you let go? What belief do you hold about God, in terms of His ability to deliver without your help?

2. When does anger show up in your soul? How does it affect others? How do you let go of the anger without sinning?

3. In what circumstances do you remain silent when you need to speak? What keeps you silent?

4. Where has anger become your armor? What wounds do you bear from your past? How do they continue to hurt you? And how do you wound others as a result?

5. How hard is it for you to sing? Songs of praise, songs of
   God's victories in your life? Who, or what, quenches your
   song? What lyrics would you pen for the song of your life?

What Mean These Stones?

Songs of faith become standing stones in our journey across the
Jordan. What song of deliverance will you sing to your loved
ones? What song highlights God's compassion for you, and for
those you cherish?

Power Up

> O my God, my soul is cast down within me;
> Therefore I will remember You from the land of the Jordan. . . .
> The Lord will command His lovingkindness in the daytime,
> And in the night His song shall be with me—
> A prayer to the God of my life.
> —Psalm 42:6, 8

Rock-Hard Truth

"It was a divine song, which Habakkuk sang, when
in the night he said, 'Although the fig tree shall not blos-
som, neither shall fruit be in the vines; the labor of the
olive shall fail, and the fields shall yield no meat; the
flock shall be cut off from the fold, and there shall be no
herd in the stalls: yet I will rejoice in the Lord, I will joy
in the God of my salvation.' No man can make a song in
the night of himself; he may attempt it, but he will find

that a song in the night must be divinely inspired. O thou
chief musician, let us not remain songless because afflic-
tion is upon us, tune thou our lips to the melody of
thanksgiving."

—Charles Spurgeon *Daily Help*[9]

Remember Me, O Lord

Lord God,
You sang the world into existence.
You sang at my birth.
You sing, even now, over me with delight,
comforting me with love songs.
Help me to hear Your words, Your melody, Your love,
and to sing Your song by heart.
May others hear the song in my soul
and fall in love with You.
Amen.

Memory Stone

For while we were still helpless,
at the right time
Christ died for the ungodly....
But God demonstrates His own love toward us,
in that while we were yet sinners,
Christ died for us.

— Romans 5:6, 8 NASB

CHAPTER FIVE

PHARAOH'S DAUGHTER:

REMEMBERING THE INTERVENTION OF GOD

It all started with my annual checkup. When the doctor asked, "Is there anything different in your life?" I shook my head, feet dangling from the exam table. "Not really. I feel a little weight in my left side. But it's probably nothing. I'm like my mom: after four children I'll never be well again."

"No, let's check out the weight you feel in your side."

Where a year ago nothing existed, this year they found a growth in my colon so large that the doctor said, "You need surgery in two weeks."

When I left his office, the doctor said, "Lois, don't worry about this. I think we might have discovered this early. And if we get it early, then there's a cure."

But I remember looking back at his assistant. Her face spoke the truth: "It's over."

Still, right away I had the "peace that passes all understanding," a peace that no one could understand, including

me. The doctor was in such a hurry to get this growth out
that he quickly found a surgeon for me, someone I didn't
even know.

My husband told the whole church and then told the
whole world on his radio program, "My wife needs your
prayers." Though the surgeon echoed my first doctor, "We
think we can help you right away," I kept remembering
the assistant's "it's all over" look. Still, God soothed me
with peace.

Seat-belted into the car, with Tony driving me to the
hospital, I felt his tension. But peace still fell over my
spirit. I should have been insane with worry. En route,
God gave me a song. I don't remember the words or the
melody, but I kept singing. That day in the car, my husband of twenty-five years looked at me in amazement
and said, "You're actually singing. We're going to the
hospital. You might have cancer. And you're singing."

The Lord intervenes and often gives us a song in those
midnight hours: "The Lord will command His loving-
kindness in the daytime, and in the night His song shall
be with me—a prayer to the God of my life" (Psalm
42:8).

Even wheeling into the prep room, I knew it might be
cancer but had total peace. And in surgery, when the
doctor was putting me to sleep, I laughed and quoted
Scripture. When they pulled out my colon to remove the
nine inches that contained the growth, the doctor said,
"It won't be like she's lost nine inches. She was born with
a longer colon."

Before I was born, when God formed me in my mother's womb, He intervened. He knew what was coming

and prepared me for it (Jeremiah 1).

My hospital room became a resting place, a place of sweet fellowship with the Lord. After checking on me daily, when the surgeon came to my room a week after the surgery, he said, "I don't know what's been going on. But something else is going on here in your room."

"Well, let me tell you what's been going on," I said. "I'm a child of God. . . ." The Lord prepared me in advance for that surgery; but He also put me in the hospital at that precise time so that I could talk to the doctor about Christ.

Then the doctor said, "It's unbelievable. When we took you in to surgery, you had cancer. But when we went under the microscope, it wasn't cancer." Today, my doctor tells me every time I see him, "You had cancer. But God healed you."

Another Daughter's Story

God is neither whimsical nor random in His involvement in the lives of His people. He provides, at just the right time, the right circumstances and people to make certain His plans are accomplished. Such is the case with our next woman.

Surrounded by handmaidens, the daughter of Pharaoh moves toward the Nile River to bathe. As the entourage progresses along the riverside, Pharaoh's daughter spots a tiny ark floating among the reeds, and orders one of her maids to retrieve it.

Bending over, the king's daughter opens the basket and sees a baby, bawling, in the bottom.

She hasn't noticed the girl, standing among the reeds at the edge of the water, until the girl comes forward and asks precociously, "Shall I go and call a nurse for you from the Hebrew women, that she may nurse the child for you?" Notice that as yet, the Egyptian woman has not announced her intention to keep the baby, rather than obey her father's edict to murder any boys of the Israelites. Yet, still she says, "Go," and directs the young girl on her mission.

When the child returns with the baby's mother, is Pharaoh's daughter aware of the cleverness of the young girl? That she has actually gone and fetched the baby's birth mother? Regardless, Pharaoh's daughter says, "Take this child away and nurse him for me, and I will give you your wages" (Exodus 2:9). She has, in a few moments, committed herself to the child's care.

It is not until he is weaned that the birth mother returns the child to the palace. If I were the baby's birth mother, I would worry that in the intervening time, the ruler's daughter has lost interest or forgotten her commitment to the baby. Their interaction was so brief, so fleeting. And yet the Scriptures tell us, "Pharaoh's daughter took him away and brought him up as her own son. And Moses was learned in all the wisdom of the Egyptians, and was mighty in words and deeds" (Acts 7:21–22).

This is miraculous, incredible evidence of the care of God to set up a perfect situation and prepare His servant perfectly for the calling of the future. God had put the perfect person in place—a woman with a ready heart.

*H*er Heart

Something very sweet and vulnerable occurs within the king's daughter in those minutes at the riverside. Bathing in the Nile may seem risqué to us now—we bathe in the privacy of our homes, behind shower curtains and closed doors, without maidens to test the water and then to hand us our towel and robe.

Yet bathing in the river was a natural event for people in those days, however unnatural it might be now. Undoubtedly the king's offspring felt safe, private, and relaxed. Her guard was down. People watched out for her and watched over her.

So when the baby's ark floated into her view, her heart was receptive. I love the compassion evident in her actions: she heard him crying, and her heart was moved. The Scriptures tell us, "So she had

compassion on him, and said, 'This is one of the Hebrews' children'"
(Exodus 2:6).

I imagine this young woman, a child of the harem, raised with a
nursery school of half brothers and half sisters, hearing the baby's
wails and resisting the temptation to pick him up. While she waits,
the cries intensify and she finally bends down, her dark hair flowing
about her shoulders, and pulls the baby into her arms. Naturally,
without thinking, she assumes *the stance:* feet slightly apart, legs
braced, hips engaged. She begins to sway from side to side, murmur-
ing, "Shhhh, shhhh, shhhh." She hums a few measures of a song she
learned in her younger years, shifts the baby to her shoulder, pats his
tiny, too-thin back. He is hungry after his river sojourn, and even at
three months tries to resituate himself so he can nurse.

The heart of Pharaoh's daughter is receptive, but she holds back
from ownership. The risks are still great.

Naming Rights

I once heard that in the early days of America, settlers held off
naming their newborn children. They waited until they felt more
certain the baby would survive the harsh, brutal circumstances of
pioneer days before bestowing a name on the child. This might have
meant two or three years. Babies and toddlers tended to be called,
generically, "Sister" or "Brother." Naming the baby lends an intimacy
and an involvement, and implies a heart commitment: I am invested
in your life, and I name you. So many children died at such young
ages that evidently the parents protected their own hearts a tiny bit
by not giving their babies a name.

Perhaps this is also the case with the daughter of Pharaoh: she
does not name the baby, nor is any name mentioned in Scripture, until the mother weans the baby and returns him to the palace. Undoubtedly the environment, to say nothing of the king's henchmen,
is not friendly to infants. Only when the baby is ready to leave his
birth mother's breast does the adoptive mother name him: Moses.

The name Moses may be a play on words, coming from a Hebrew word that sounds like "draw out." A perfect name for the child

who was drawn out of the waters of the Nile, and a perfect prophecy and promise for the man who would one day draw his people out of Egypt and into freedom.

How reassuring to know that regardless of how far someone might be from the kingdom, she can still play a part in the redemption of a people. Though she likely worshiped false gods, the princess was a vital link in the true God's chain of events that would deliver a nation from bondage.

*H*er Lineage

As for the daughter of the reigning king, we have no mention of her name. She is likely one of many daughters of the harem, with half-royal blood running through her veins. But the lack of a name does not undermine the significance of the gift this unnamed woman gave the Israelites, and ultimately gave us: she preserved the life of the one who would rescue a nation from slavery. A nation out of which the Savior of the world would come.

Even without a name, even without a royal mother, she is royalty, because of the way God worked through her life and situation.

Find the gift of your childhood, your parentage, and invite God to redeem the lost, the stolen, the painful times.

Is this not so for you as well? You may not know your birth mother. Or you do know her: she raised you, but ugliness and pain occurred. Perhaps your childhood was not a close, happy, safe, dreaming time with loving parents. Do not underestimate the pain you experienced.

But do not overvalue it either. Do not use it as an excuse to be less than who God has planned for you to be. Every person in your life plays a significant part in shaping you, preparing you for your future. Find the gift of your childhood, your parentage, and invite God to redeem the lost, the stolen, the painful times. To create a passageway over the rivers you will need to cross to do His work as His daughter in this world.

$\mathcal{H}$er Wisdom

This daughter of the king intuits the right way to handle this sudden development: an infant is floating in the waters, is hungry, and is supposed to be dead as per the king's orders. It baffles me that she saves this beautiful baby and then immediately sends him off to a wet nurse to be raised on breast milk until weaned. And yet, since it was customary in wealthy or royal families to hire out the feeding of their babies, this is a natural and normal response for her. Babies get in the way of a heavy social life. Blue bloods do not demean themselves or tie themselves down to the rigorous schedule of a nursing infant, nor the inconvenience of swollen breasts and dripping milk.

Still, this child is not her own flesh and blood. She is under no obligation to save his life or even to prolong it. In fact, she also is under orders from the king: "So Pharaoh commanded all his people, saying, 'Every son who is born you shall cast into the river'" (Exodus 1:22). Clearly, from somewhere deep within, this daughter embraces life, and her feminine heart cries out for the baby's well-being. He is orphaned; he is hungry; he needs to eat. And this too plays into God's hand and plans. His plans for Moses, his plans for Moses' birth family—what craziness! A slave mother paid to nurse her own baby! And even crazier, a baby who is supposed to have drowned, but whose life is saved by the daughter of the very king who ordained the boy's death.

How can you not love a God who so intimately and so wildly oversees the details of one person's salvation?

Isn't this true for you as well? God has played a personal role in bringing you to this place, at this time, putting exactly the right people in your life at precisely the right moments. Maybe it wasn't the daughter of a king—or was it? All along the riverside of your life, God has stationed people whose words, or actions, or kindness, or wisdom guided you, filled a need in you, prepared you in some way for the future. And God's intervention is as recent as this moment, and as long ago as generations.

Once, after dropping the younger children off at school, fear nearly blindsided me. I had struggled with fear earlier in our marriage, but this was different. My hands literally shook on the steering wheel, and I had to pull over. "Lord, what is this?" I asked. I knew something was wrong.

Our oldest daughter, who was away at college, came to mind. "Oh, God," I prayed, "don't tell me she is pregnant." Then God started pouring Scriptures into my thoughts: 1 Corinthians 10:13; Philippians 4; Romans 8:28. The Lord started to minister to me, and I had church right there on the side of the road.

He prepared me in advance, so when, two weeks later, her phone call came, letting me know she indeed was pregnant, I was able to be a strong source of encouragement and comfort to her.

How do you recognize God's intervening hand in your life? In *The God Hunt*, Karen Mains suggests four ways to perceive God's active presence:

1. *Any obvious answer to prayer*
2. *Any unexpected evidence of his care*
3. *Any help to do God's work in the world*
4. *Any unusual linkage or timing.*[10]

Karen suggests that we remember and honor these moments, crafting them into stories to be told around our tables, with our families, with our friends. That we remember. So others may know that this God is a God who takes an intimate and personal interest in our lives.

ℋer Power

Regardless of Pharaoh's dictate, this woman has the power to save life or to take life. And even though she may not have the full power of a full-blooded princess, she has enough power to say yes to life when it appears in the middle of her bathing routine.

Her power is limited: she will not likely ever be queen, will not likely marry a prince, will not ever reign over the kingdom or sit on a throne. But she has the power to reign over her own life and the lives of those she influences. This woman knows that she can adopt whom she chooses. And, common sense and king's edicts aside, she chooses Moses.

Yes, her power is limited. But it is enough.

When we sync in to God's plan, then our teeny power is irrelevant. In fact, our power to impact change is minimal to nil when we try to work on our own strength. We are like AAA batteries in a penlight, compared to God's stadium lights. But when we plug into God's power, when we tap into His lines, God's power becomes our power. If we have enough power left to invite God's power to take over, it is enough power.

When do you feel weak? When do you feel powerless? When do you feel ineffective? Take note of those times. And thank God for them. For the Lord says to you, as He said to Paul, "My grace is sufficient for you, for My strength is made perfect in weakness" (2 Corinthians 12:9). In the same verse, Paul goes on to say, "Most gladly I will rather boast in my infirmities, that the power of Christ may rest upon me." Jesus said, "Without Me you can do nothing" (John 15:5).

*You can refuse the darkness and look
for the pinprick of light, look for the
good in a bad situation, choose to see
God's hand in rock-hard times instead
of turning your back on Him.*

If we can do it on our own, it is probably not worth doing. Praise God for that. And ask for His power to live the life He has placed before you. Even if that includes a river too high and too deep to ford.

Naming Power

But we are not powerless. From the beginning of the world, God designated naming rights to human beings. "Out of the ground the Lord God formed every beast of the field and every bird of the air, and brought them to Adam to see what he would call them. And whatever Adam called each living creature, that was its name" (Genesis 2:19). Placing a name on something or someone indicates authority.

You too have naming power: the ability to speak into a situation, to call forth life from that place. You have the power to refuse to be an Eeyore, who famously said, "Tut tut, it looks like rain." You have the power to refuse any doomsday-prophet syndromes. You can refuse the darkness and look for the pinprick of light, look for the good in a bad situation, choose to see God's hand in rock-hard times instead of turning your back on Him.

You can call forth the positive qualities in someone intent on misbehaving. Sue does this with her prodigal child. She sees him going in the wrong direction, and while she addresses his sin, she also says, "This is not who you really are. You are a young man with a good heart, a child who was sensitive to injustice, who cried when a mouse got caught in a trap. Even as a boy, you served others less fortunate than yourself. Remember when you fixed Johnny's bike tire because he didn't have a daddy to do it for him?" Even though her son has gotten lost in bad habits, Sue reminds him of who he is, so that he can begin to find himself again.

Sue has naming power.

So do you. You can refuse to buckle to negativism, refuse to have a bad day, refuse to be pessimistic. You can say, sing, shout out, "This is the day the Lord has made; I will rejoice and be glad in it" (see Psalm 118:24). Say it until you believe it, and then live in the joy of that amazing truth.

That's naming power.

*W*aters of Life

The waters that were intended to kill life ("Drown the baby boys!") become waters of life as the daughter of the earthly king draws Moses from the water.

So it is with your life, with your River Jordan. The Enemy—the paranoid, wicked ruler of this age—wants the waters to take your life, to drown you, to see your tiny ark overturned. But the heavenly King's Son watches by the side of the river, waiting for just the right moment to intervene, to rescue you, to convey upon you all that you will need to live this life well until you cross the river that final time.

Travel Mercies

1. What anonymity do you feel in terms of your role in this world? In terms of God's care of you?

2. No one has a perfect childhood. Describe some of the pain you have experienced. The disappointments, losses, hurts. How do you overvalue those times? How do they stop you from moving forward? What is the gift of your childhood, your parentage? Invite God to redeem the lost, the stolen, the painful times. Do not use them as excuses to be less than who God has planned for you to be.

3. Where do you see divine timing and intervention in your life?

4. Every person in your life plays a significant part in shaping you, preparing you for your future. How might the people who have disappointed or wounded you have played a role in your shaping, in your becoming the woman God intended?

5. Where do you feel powerless? How can you sync into God's power? How can you name the situation in faith, believing that God will bring good out of hardship and help your heart to reflect His face?

What Mean These Stones?

How did God intervene in your life this past week? This past year? Where can you see His hand, carefully weaving circumstances and people into just the right position to impact your heart? How can you share your stories with others?

Power Up

"But as for you, you meant evil against me; but God meant it for good, in order to bring it about as it is this day, to save many people alive."

—Genesis 50:20

Rock-Hard Truth

God can use the cries of a baby to touch the heart of a woman to change the course of a nation. Surely He can do this in your life as well.

—Jane Rubietta

Remember Me, O Lord

Oh, Lord,
You had Your eye on me when I was but a babe;
when I was forming in my mother's womb,
You ordained my days.
You knew the people who would draw me from the waters of the rivers,
the waters that would threaten my life and future.
You knew the people whose interest would help shape
who I am becoming.

Thank You for overseeing all the days of my life.
Help me to recognize Your intervention
and to move over the waters of this next flooding river.
You are able.
You are my bridge.
Thank You!
Amen.

Memory Stone

*Therefore He is also able
to save to the uttermost
those who come to God through Him,
since He always lives
to make intercession for them.*

— *Hebrews 7:25*

CHAPTER SIX

ZIPPORAH:

REMEMBERING THE INTERCESSION OF GOD

Their stories spilled out after she locked the door on her boyfriend. Her children crowded behind her, fear and relief a strange combination on their faces. She turned toward them, her back against the door, and drew them into her arms. Through tears, they confirmed what she suspected: her boyfriend, their father, had abused them physically and sexually.

All her might rose up within her, and she vowed to fight for their healing and their lives. She fought for counseling for them, fought the judge when their father took her to court for shared custody. And when her heart broke in the night, when her sins of negligence and self-centeredness choked her, she confessed them before God, knowing that Christ stood in the gap for her. God's forgiveness strengthened her to awaken the next morning, face down the demons of shame, and again intercede for her children.

𝒜nother Fight, Another Intercession

The seven sisters jostle and joke as they lead their sheep to the watering troughs. Heat shimmers in the wilderness of Midian, and both sisters and sheep feel it. Shepherds arrive and crowd them, bullying them, trying to drive the shepherdesses away. None of them notice the lone foreigner sitting by the well until he rises with commanding authority and comes to their rescue, running off the shepherds and then watering the girls' herd.

The girls arrive home early from the fields. Their father, the priest of Midian, asks his daughters, "Why have you returned so early today?"

"An Egyptian rescued us from the shepherds. He even drew water for us and watered the flock."

"And where is he? Why did you leave him? Invite him to have something to eat."

Over dinner, perhaps, the Egyptian reveals his true identity: Moses, an Israelite, son of Amram and Jochebed, adopted son of Pharaoh's daughter. Whatever the prince-like foreigner says, it is enough to eventually convince Reuel (also called Jethro) to give his daughter Zipporah to Moses in marriage (see Exodus 2:15–21).

And so begins Zipporah's journey at the side of Moses. While he would be the one to draw the Israelites out of Egypt, God will use her to draw the past out of Moses, and to ultimately preserve his life through her own quick thinking and courage.

𝒵ipporah's Rescue

As one of seven sisters, Zipporah may be top in the pecking order of siblings because she is the one who gets the husband. Daughters were rarely shepherdesses in those days unless there were no boys in the family,[11] so the girls walked the fields, tended the wounds of their flocks, protected them from enemies, herded them to green pastures. These must have been strong women, lifting heavy animals and hauling buckets of water. Shepherdesses needed to be willing to defend their sheep, and so could likely wield a rock or a stick to ward off predators.

But Zipporah cannot save herself from the bully-shepherds who try to push her and her sisters away from the well. Her defenses are not that strong. What amazing timing that "the Egyptian," who is actually an Israelite named Moses, arrives at the well and rests there, unseen by either group, and only makes his presence known when he is needed.

I wonder about that—Moses has just run through the desert after intervening in a fight, a fight that went desperately wrong, ending in murder and costing him his citizenship and adopted family (Exodus 2:15). Does he hesitate to get involved? Does he argue with himself as he watches the gang assert their supposed superiority over the seven girls?

And how does Zipporah feel, strong, wilderness-smart Zipporah, as she realizes that she cannot save herself or her sisters from these desert thugs? It is good to know when you need help, and she knows. It is good to be able to be rescued.

Women today are coached and coaxed to be independent and without needs: we aren't supposed to need help, to need someone to carry the groceries or push the wheelbarrow or help us balance monstrous tasks. We are supposed to be able to do everything men can do on top of everything women already do.

My friend works from her home office, overseeing the entire household and a sixty-hour-per-week job. In the midst of a crushing deadline, with piles of work and piles of laundry and piles of dust and no food in the house and a trip for work looming, she leaned against her desk with weariness. Her husband came into the room at that moment and asked, "How can I help?"

She surveyed her empire from her desk and ran through the list of chores ahead of her. She didn't want him to fix dinner because he wouldn't do it right. She didn't want him to do the laundry because he always folded the towels wrong and washed reds and whites together. She didn't want him to go to the store because he would buy things they didn't need and couldn't afford.

So she said, "I'll be fine. I'll take care of it. Thanks, though."

Her husband shook his head, his face drawn and sad. "You don't need me anymore, do you?"

His words were her wake-up call. It is good to be able to be helped, whether by a husband or by a friend or a stranger. Don't buy into the lie of this world that you should be totally independent and need no one. Beware of your strength leading to too much independence where you are not able to receive help.

Zipporah knows she needs to be rescued, and that this foreigner is the one to do it. God has provided him for such a time as this.

It is good to be able to be rescued.

Not everyone has a problem with being rescued. Michelle cannot seem to do anything without a panicked phone call to her husband. When the kids are sick, she needs for him to stay home with her. When they need to visit the doctor, she can't manage the two of them at the same time, so he takes off work again.

Beware of constantly needing to be rescued. What lurks at the bottom of that need?

This may be cleverly disguised power: when Michelle calls and he jumps, then she knows she runs the show. She measures his love for her by his ability and availability to rescue. Her helplessness may actually be manipulation and control.

Serious Healing

Moses rescues Zipporah at the well, and she rescues him from a life of running. There is no doubt in my mind that Zipporah marries a man who needs serious healing. He was taken from his birth mother after being weaned, and raised by people who worship false gods. No mention is ever made of an adoptive father. He received the education of a king's son and perhaps lost the faith of his childhood. He has a teensy problem with anger, as we see in Exodus 2:12 when he happens upon an Egyptian beating a Hebrew: "So he looked this way and that way, and when he saw no one, he killed the Egyptian and hid him in the sand." After committing murder, he runs for his life. He is a refugee on top of his other problems. A man on the run.

Zipporah marries a man with a past. Beneath his princely bearing and fine speech lives an imperfect man with painful chapters in his life—chapters that helped shape him. This is true for us as well: our painful chapters help shape us. We get to choose whether the pain will shape us into someone who changes the world for the better, as Moses and Zipporah did. God is well able to transform that pain, to convert pain into a scalpel that will carve us into the image of Christ. We become who God intended us to be when we embrace our pain and allow it to sculpt us. We've known rock-hard places, but refuse to allow our hearts to turn to stone because of our past, or our loved one's past. Instead, we give God artistic license to sculpt what He will from our pain.

*We get to choose whether the pain
will shape us into someone who changes
the world for the better.*

None of us knows exactly what we are getting into when we marry our "prince." If we did, if we realized how much our blemishes would show up and how much our spouse's flaws and failings would bother us, if we understood how hard it is to commit to a relationship and stick it out and make it work, who would go through with it? And Moses, of course, married an imperfect woman with a past too.

Join the crowd. We all have a past, and all the people who crowd our lives and line the margins of our streets have a past. There is method to the apparent madness of our lives.

Midian means "brawling, contention, discord, strife." This seems a likely place for the brawling Moses to flee. Certainly he ran into a crowd of brawling shepherds while he waited at the well. Surely Zipporah was no stranger to contention, discord, and strife with six sisters and lots of sheep. In fact, Midian could describe anywhere on earth, anyplace people inhabit.

When Moses escaped to Midian, God divinely put him into this family. God used Zipporah and her family to begin Moses' long, healing journey back to his own heart and back to the God of his childhood, and to prepare him for his future as one of the mightiest men who would ever live.

I grew up in an obscure place in South America, out in the "boonies." And yet into my own middle of nowhere God decided to bring a revival, and the handsome young man sent to make preparations was named Tony Evans. He showed up at my door one day, and we ended up ministering together during the event. Later, I lived for a long time obscure in marriage. We learned to rescue each other with our strengths and weaknesses. We learned, in our obscure place, to meet the needs of the partnership God had called us to.

Maybe you feel like you are in an obscure place, living off in the middle of nowhere, or anonymously dwelling in a crowd, with no particular gifts or talents. Moses felt like that when God called him from the burning bush. And into Moses' doubts, God spoke, "What's that in your hand?"

"A stick."

"Throw it down, Moses." And the stick became a serpent.

Whatever is in your hand, throw it down. Concentrate on what God wants to do with what you have in your hand. He has a plan. There are people in your life whom you can impact for their good and God's glory. The witness of a person who has experienced God's healing and tells others of it changes the world, one story at a time. And who knows? The person you invest in may one day become someone God uses to do mighty Moses-like works.

Zipporah couldn't see the future—couldn't possibly know that her prince of a husband would one day, in a breathtaking display of leadership and courage, defy one of the primary world powers and lead two million people out of slavery. She could only love her husband, one day at a time, and choose to invest in this man God stationed at a well for their mutual rescue.

So it is with you. There are people in your world—brawling, contentious, obnoxious people—who may look good but have a messed-up interior life. How can you be a willing partner in God's sculpting process? How can you love the other, one day at a time, with a faith that will not let go?

*T*he Process Continues

We get a sneak preview of God's good work in this family when the first child is born. Moses calls him Gershom, "I have been a stranger in a foreign land" (Exodus 2:22). Though he has a new family—six sisters, a wife, a priest for a father—his exile is uppermost in his mind. His wounds show up in his firstborn son's name. "I have been a stranger; I haven't known anyone here; I have been alone."

But as a result of his new relatives and God's work through them, Moses is able to name his second son Eliezer, "The God of my father was my help" (Exodus 18:4). Moses has gone from mourning his alien, runaway status to claiming that the one true God is his helper. That is remarkable progress.

This encourages me to hold on to those I love, those in whom I invest time and prayer and friendship, while God continues to do mutual work in our heart and character. Zipporah holds on to this relationship, continues to love her strong-minded husband, who sprinted away from his past with so much emotional baggage that it's a wonder he didn't trip and fall and never get up again.

Forty years after Moses runs away from Pharaoh and toward Zipporah's arms, God meets with her husband on the mountain where he is tending sheep. Moses receives the commission from God to return to Egypt and command Pharaoh to "Let My people go." At age eighty, Moses is finally ready. The wilderness years have done good work on Zipporah's husband. The years have wrought healing in his heart, and, with God's help, he is ready to traverse the wilderness yet again. He returns home to pack up his wife and children.

A Faith Like Flint, a Heart of Love

Zipporah doesn't lose herself in the process of being married to a mighty man, a strong, brilliant, educated man. Though she must at least be in her fifties by now, Zipporah still shows the spunk of the shepherdess. She hops on a donkey, determined to accompany Moses, and they plod to Egypt (Exodus 4:19–20). She believes in Moses, believes in his relationship with God, and though she may have questions, she prepares to journey at his side.

But the Lord has another word for the man who would set His people free. To prepare Moses for his role in the exodus as a mighty man of God, something is lacking.

Years ago, God had spoken to their forefather, Abraham, saying,

> "This is My covenant which you shall keep, between Me and you and your descendants after you: Every male child among you shall be circumcised . . . in the flesh of your foreskins. . . . My covenant shall be in your flesh for an everlasting covenant. And the uncircumcised male child . . . shall be cut off from his people; he has broken My covenant" (see Genesis 17:10–14).

God wants holiness in His children, and if He is going to be present through us to change the world, then He has to take care of business. Evidently, Moses has unfinished business because God meets the family en route and seeks "to kill him" (Exodus 4:24).

Zipporah swings into action. She grabs a flint knife, a wedge of sharp rock, and quickly circumcises their son, setting on him and thus on their entire family the sign of God's covenant with them.

Consider this: she and Moses have been married for nearly forty years; this son is not a newborn. He is likely an adult, and this is a very personal procedure. Zipporah knows herself so well, and knows her God so intimately, that she does not hesitate to do what is right. She has what it takes to do what is necessary: take up the rock tool and set aside her son for God. Her rock-hard faith, born in rock-hard places, enables her to do the hard thing.

This is not about circumcision; this is about the heart. It isn't the circumcision that saved Moses, or his family, or all his ancestors before and descendants after him; it was the heart compliance with an external sign that said, "I belong to God." And so it is with us: God commands us to circumcise our hearts; to cut into the excess flesh—the places where sin easily grows—and to demonstrate that circumcision by the way we live. We are to be set apart for God, living lives that reflect His holiness and goodness and love. Paul sums this up in Galatians 5:6: "For in Christ Jesus neither circumcision nor uncircumcision has any value. The only thing that counts is faith expressing itself through love" (NIV).

The apostle goes on to say, "Serve one another in love. The entire law is summed up in a single command: 'Love your neighbor as yourself'" (Galatians 5:13–14 NIV). Loving others proves the circumcision of our hearts. Our relationship with God will show up in how we love our neighbor as ourselves.

Long ago, when I dreaded going to church because of some people I felt didn't like me, Tony said, "Just focus on the people who love you when you go down that aisle." The loving people in my life have enabled me to love those my mother called "peculiar people," the unlovely ones.

> LOVE ONE ANOTHER
> ❖ Spend time with people different from you, so you can learn to love and appreciate them.
> ❖ Focus on the other person.
> ❖ Ask yourself, "What does love mean? What is best for the other person? How can I love her?"

This convicts me (Jane). I am too busy to love my neighbors very well. I am polite and kind if I meet them on the street and actually recognize them; I try to wave at them if I notice them in their SUVs. Sometimes my closest neighbor is the person sitting next to me on the plane, or the woman with the squalling children fighting over treats in the checkout lane at the grocery store.

Busyness is not a sign of our godliness. Frankly, our busyness is often part of the excess flesh and sin in our lives. When we are too busy to love, we short-circuit God's very means for drawing others to Himself.

What will it take, once you have given your heart to Jesus? How

will He circumcise your heart? What would it look like for your faith
to express itself in love?

𝒫ower in the Blood

This mysterious story continues when Zipporah takes the foreskin and touches her husband's feet with it, saying, "Surely you are a
bridegroom of blood to me" (Exodus 4:25 NIV).

It will be only a brief time until her husband appears before
Pharaoh, and because of the ruler's stubbornness, Moses will call
down ten plagues on him, his country, and his people. The final
plague, the death of the firstborn, can only be prevented if the Israelites take the blood of a lamb without blemish, a firstborn lamb,
and smear it over their doors and the doorposts (Exodus 12:4–11).

The Lord then tells the Israelites, "Now the blood shall be a sign
for you on the houses where you are. And when I see the blood, I will
pass over you; and the plague shall not be on you to destroy you,"
(12:13).

This instituted what Jewish people even today observe as
Passover, where they remember their captivity in Egypt and God's
miraculous deliverance of them from slavery, and commemorate
when the spirit of death hovered over the land and passed over those
with the blood on the doorframe. The Lord later tells us in Hebrews,
"Without the shedding of blood there is no forgiveness" (9:22 NIV).

And so this leads us to Christ, the firstborn Son of God, who
without sin or blemish gave up His life. His blood eliminated once
and for all the need for circumcision to save us. His blood, His perfect blood, stops the plague of death over any who call on His name.
His blood brings forgiveness, the forgiveness for which Moses hun-
gered as he ran from his past.

We too long for this forgiveness. This longing lies beneath our
busyness, beneath our ruined relationships and rocky journey as we
try to escape our past and even our present. This very Jesus becomes
our future and our hope as we look to Him for our very life. When we
claim Christ's blood for our own forgiveness, He becomes our Savior.

*I*ntercession

With Moses' *past*, with his *present* as he learns to leave behind the shame of his youth, and with his *future*, Zipporah stands by his side. Zipporah means "bird," and just as he flew to Midian for refuge, she flies to his rescue with the foreskin circumcision. She intercedes for Moses, wedging herself into the tight crevice between life and death, standing in the gap between him and God.

And even so Christ stands in the gap for us, interceding for us, wedging Himself between us and God, creating a bridge over which we can walk into relationship with Him once again. Free—no longer a slave to sin, no longer encumbered by the flesh of brokenness.

And God calls us, even as He called Zipporah, to intercede for others. Your neighbor stands at a flooding river, just as you do. Through your love, you can become a bridge that takes her to God.

And the rivers will not overcome you.

Travel Mercies

1. When have you needed to be rescued? Who was there for you? In general, what is it like when someone attempts to rescue you? Is that difficult to allow, or do you thrive on rescue, always needing someone to bail you out? What is behind either reaction?

2. Where do you need to give God "artistic license" to sculpt beauty from your rocky past and the painful terrain of your life? How can you embrace your pain and allow God to shape you through it?

3. What will it take, once you have given your heart to Jesus? How will He circumcise your heart? In other words, where is sin clogging your heart, standing in the way of your relationship with God and with others? Ask the Lord to reveal the places where you need forgiveness, need freedom, need cleansing. What would it look like for your faith to express itself in love?

4. Who has stood in the gap for you, as Zipporah did for Moses? Invite God to show you where in your life others have been there for you, people you might not even have recognized at the time.

5. How does God want to use you in your closest relationships? How does God want you to be a safe place, a healing place, for others? Where is God calling you to stand in the gap for others?

What Mean These Stones?

Christ's blood stops the plague of death in your life. Have you invited Him to do this, receiving His sacrifice? If not, confess your sin, your need of "circumcision," and simply ask Jesus to save you with His blood. Then, just as the Israelites celebrated the Passover, how will you celebrate His passing-over your sins? How will you frame the stories of your salvation for others?

Power Up

Blessed is he whose transgressions are forgiven,
whose sins are covered. . . .
I acknowledged my sin to you
and did not cover up my iniquity.
I said, "I will confess my transgressions to the Lord"—
and you forgave the guilt of my sin.
Therefore let everyone who is godly pray to you
while you may be found;
surely when the mighty waters rise,
they will not reach him."

—Psalm 32:1, 5-6 NIV

Rock-Hard Truth

My hope is built on nothing less
Than Jesus' blood and righteousness;
I dare not trust the sweetest frame,
But wholly lean on Jesus' name.

On Christ the solid rock I stand—
All other ground is sinking sand,
All other ground is sinking sand.
—"The Solid Rock"

Remember Me, O Lord

Father God,
The river is high where I stand right now.
The floodwaters creep toward me,
eating away at the solid ground on which I stand.
And yet, there is no water too deep for You,
no river too wide,
no sin too large,
no problem too overwhelming.
Take me to the rock that is higher than I,
and rescue me.
Stand in the gap for me;
be a bridge over the troubling waters,
that I may declare Your praise.
In Jesus' name, who stands in the gap.
Amen.

Memory Stone

For You have been
a shelter for me,
A strong tower
from the enemy.
I will abide in Your tabernacle
forever;
I will trust in the shelter
of Your wings.

— *Psalm 61:3-4*

CHAPTER SEVEN

RAHAB:

REMEMBERING THE HOSPITALITY OF GOD

Rachel lost her virginity in college. Too much to drink, too much false intimacy. The day after one of those nights, over coffee with her best friend, she said, "I have ruined it. What if I get pregnant? I don't even know this guy except through my history class."

Both young women carried a history of sexual experimentation. Both of them were wounded by touch, unhealthy touch, from people who were supposed to care for them. Rachel was a child of divorce, and her friend had experienced abandonment through her parents' addictions.

Then a woman on campus welcomed them into her life. Through her, these two friends encountered hospitality that accepted them as they were, with no judgment of their past. They learned about Jesus Christ and began to experience what it meant to be truly saved: saved from their brokenness, saved from their mistakes, saved from their past and their sin.

*The friends stood up in one another's weddings, and
each bride wore white as she stepped down the runner to
take her place beside her groom. These young women
were new virgins, the stains of their past washed clean by
Christ.*

A Strange Hospitality

Terror settles like silt over the community of two thousand people. Animals move restlessly, stamping their feet, shifting. The walls of the town are thick but not thick enough for the mighty war-god coming their way. All strangers are regarded with suspicion, the possibility of enemy spies a very real danger.

Rahab answers the pounding on her door. Two men stand outside. Perhaps they are would-be clients. Her trade is prostitution, and men regularly trek to her home in the wall of the city. As she ushers them in, she learns that they are spies (so much for secrecy in reconnaissance!) sent from the vagabond Hebrew nation to check out the city of Jericho.

Vigilant neighbors spot the men, however. A leak alerts the king of Jericho: "Behold, men have come here tonight from the children of Israel to search out the country" (Joshua 2:2). He dispatches a party to investigate.

This batch of men tramp to the door as well, saying, "Bring out the men who have come to you, who have entered your house, for they have come to search out all the country" (v. 3).

But Rahab has hidden the spies. For some reason, the king's consort don't search her home, but believe her response, "Yes, the men came to me, but I did not know where they were from. And it happened as the gate was being shut, when it was dark, that the men went out. Where the men went I do not know; pursue them quickly, for you may overtake them" (vv. 4–5).

The search party rushes after the spies, racing along the road to the fords of the Jordan River. The gates of the city clang shut behind them.

Darting to the rooftop, Rahab pulls up stalks of flax and un-covers the spies. She recounts what she knows, what she has heard, what she by faith believes: "I know that the Lord has given you the land, that the terror of you has fallen on us, and that all the inhabi-tants of the land are fainthearted because of you."

Word has traveled of their God's exploits: the drying up of the Red Sea, the destruction of the Amorite kings. "As soon as we heard these things, our hearts melted; neither did there remain any more courage in anyone because of you, for the Lord your God, He is God in heaven above and on earth beneath" (vv. 8–11).

Rahab wisely strikes a deal with the spies. She could easily turn them over to the search party and possibly win some favor or lever-age in the king's eyes. But since she saved the lives of the spies, lying for them and diverting the authorities, she begs, "Swear to me by the Lord . . . that you also will show kindness to my father's house, and give me a true token, and spare my father, my mother, my brothers, my sisters, and all that they have, and deliver our lives from death" (vv. 12–13).

They reach terms of agreement, and Rahab lowers them from the window on the outer wall of the city, devising an escape plan for them. Then, in order for the Hebrew warriors to recognize her home, she ties the scarlet rope in the window as a plea for her fami-ly's salvation.

The Heart of Prostitution

Les Miserables, the award-winning musical based on Victor Hugo's book, depicts the downward spiral of Fantine, a woman caught in poverty, abandoned by her lover, left with a daughter she desperately loves. When she loses her job because she refuses the sexual advances of her boss, she ends up unemployed and on the street. Frantic to care for her child, she turns to prostitution.

The song "Lovely Ladies" depicts the truth of those caught in the destructive spin of prostitution:

"Lovely ladies
Lying on a bed
Just as well they never see
The hate that's in your head
Don't they know they're
Making love to one already
Dead?"[12]

Beneath the lyrics lies a deep truth: prostitutes have died, one unhealthy touch at a time. According to Genesis House, a nonprofit ministry to prostitutes in Chicago, 90–95 percent of female prostitutes were sexually abused as children. Because of their abuse, their self-worth is so low they expect poor treatment from others and easily end up in abusive relationships with men.

$\mathcal{T}$he desire for unfailing love is
God-given so we will be God-driven.

It often happens like this: A woman who doesn't think she can do any better gets in a relationship with a man who treats her terribly. *He really loves me,* she thinks, *so this is okay.* The result is much the same for the 5–10 percent of prostitutes who were not victims of child sexual abuse. She also goes along with sex, then drugs, then sells herself because he tells her, "You gotta bring in some money for us." And of course, she needs to support the drug habit he helped her acquire. All along, she keeps trying to convince herself that he loves her.[13]

The longing to be loved is universal. It is seeded in our hearts by God, who wants to love us with a depth unlike anyone on earth. We are created out of love, for love. The Scriptures tell us that, "What a [person] desires is unfailing love" (Proverbs 19:22 NIV). The desire for unfailing love is God-given so we will be God-driven.

But this need for love is easily twisted: by our families, by our society, by Hollywood, and by advertising moguls. A sense of worthlessness and invisibility dictates, and women who are abused may feel that touch, even unhealthy touch, validates them: "Though it may hurt, I am real because you touch me."

Recovery from prostitution involves many layers of help: physical, psychological, spiritual, and educational. Not only are prostitutes often mothers,[14] with very real physical needs in terms of housing for themselves and their children, but they also may have a variety of medical issues that need to be addressed. Psychologically, finding healing begins with addressing the issues that brought them to the streets—and national statistics point out that the average age of those entering prostitution is fourteen.[15]

Among other things, this means that many women involved left school long before walking across a stage for a diploma. Education, not only about their issues and choices, but also about how to help them survive legitimately in the world without abusing themselves to stay alive, becomes essential. But ultimately, without a spiritual new beginning, a prostitute will miss the best hope and future available. This is what the Hebrew reconnaissance team who pound on Rahab's door offer her: a new beginning.

Rahab's Situation

Preachers often paint Rahab as scheming, manipulative, lying, and self-centered, out to save her own skin. She finds herself in good company, frankly. Who of us hasn't been each of those things? Didn't Jesus, speaking to the religious people who wanted to stone an adulteress, say, "He who is without sin among you, let him throw a stone at her first" (John 8:7)? As with the midwives, we find ourselves again asking the question, "What about the lies?" And again, we have to choose when our actions will save lives or when they will destroy lives. She lies in order to save lives. She knows the situation is much bigger than her doorway and her home in the wall of the city.

But let's look behind the stereotype. Given current research, it's possible that Rahab was victimized by sexual abuse as a child, likely by someone close to her. It's also possible she had children. And because of the nature of human brokenness, we can assume that when she answered the door to find Israelite soldiers outside, she carried within her significant pain and long-term wounds.

Who can judge her motives in welcoming these men? What we do know is that she, though a very unsafe and possibly unsavory woman, provided a safe place for them. When the troop came to the door looking for these spies, she hid the spies, lied to the search squad, and then sent off the Hebrews with a plan for their safe return to camp.

The stories of their God preceded the scouts: she remembers these stories aloud and comes to a place of trust in this God. Verbalizing the truth about the God of the Hebrews moves her faith forward.

*H*all of Faith, Cloud of Witnesses

Rahab's immense courage isn't apparent, perhaps, to people in our times. We average citizens in this era haven't lived through the nightmare of invasions and armies conquering our cities, then destroying our homeland. But spies from our country who trade secrets to other countries are not treated kindly, nor are those who harbor spies.

The God of heaven and earth is on the move, and Rahab wants to be part of that process.

Even so, Rahab makes the decision to shelter the spies, in spite of possible consequences either from the spies themselves or from her hometown security. The king could easily kill her for her traitorous actions, but she sees the larger picture: the God of heaven and earth is on the move, and she wants to be part of that process. With her life totally unsafe already, she has little to lose and much to gain.

And so we read in Hebrews 11:31, "By faith the harlot Rahab did not perish with those who did not believe, when she had received the spies with peace."

Her welcome extends *peace* to the spies. Enemies are advancing; the great war-god is on the move; troops are pounding on her door. This is hardly peaceful. And Rahab does not strike me as a person of peace, but rather an extremely conflicted woman.

But notice also the context of the verse in Hebrews: the thirty preceding verses detail the faith of spiritual heavyweights. The chapter lifts up Abel, Enoch, Noah, Abraham, Sarah, Isaac, Jacob, Joseph, and Moses as examples of people who trusted God even though the result was not yet seen. In fact, Hebrews 11 opens with, "Now faith is the substance of things hoped for, the evidence of things not seen."

Further, these giants of the faith lived comparatively godly lives. They hauled around after God for years, taking enormous risks. And yet, Rahab is included in the documentary of belief. She, a woman marred by the sexual sin and abuse of others and by her own desperate choices, wounded by life in a harsh world, gets posted in the spiritual "Who's Who" of Hebrews. All she really wants, she thinks, are safety and deliverance.

God's dreams for us are so much larger than ours. God has higher plans for Rahab than just safety. Because of her faith in Him, because she dares to extend safety to spies in exchange for her own life, this prostitute is called one of the "great cloud of witnesses" in Hebrews 12:1.

She welcomes the spies and becomes a witness to the grace and peace of God. Talk about transformation. Talk about an amazing God who can take us at our very worst, our most degraded and shameful, and shape us toward His image.

The Hospitality of God

This woman, who was used to her hospitality being abused, whose very body had become a "home" for too many men, who had abused her femininity to make it through her days and to make ends meet—this woman creates space for God to act by welcoming the spies into her home.

How fitting, how like God, that Rahab's name means "roomy, broad, large, at liberty"; and we see her heart expand beyond her own ends as she makes room for these men. She, the abused and ashamed, invites others into refuge and safety.

And as a result, when the Hebrew soldiers torch the town, they save Rahab and her family. They lead her out of the red-light district and carry her away from the doomed Jericho. The Scriptures tell us that ultimately the nation of Israel made room for her within its community.

The first chapter of Matthew begins, "A record of the genealogy of Jesus Christ the Son of David, the son of Abraham" (v. 1 NIV). Matthew then traces Christ's lineage on Joseph's side, beginning with Abraham and moving generations later to, "Salmon the father of Boaz, whose mother was *Rahab*, Boaz the father of Obed, whose mother was Ruth, Obed the father of Jesse, and Jesse the father of King David" (1:5–6 NIV, emphasis mine). If we follow the family line, we come to the great miracle: "and Jacob the father of Joseph, the husband of Mary, of whom was born Jesus, who is called the Christ" (v. 16 NIV).

Wait. Let's hear that again: Rahab the prostitute is the great-great-great-great paternal grandmother of Jesus Christ, the Son of God, our Savior and Redeemer. God made room for Rahab in the lineage of the great kings of Judah, and the one true King! What a display of full forgiveness: God has bought back this harlot, this person who sold her body as a way of life; the Lord has purchased her from the degradation of prostitution. Though once she was lost, God found her and gave her new life. Truly Rahab can say,

> Though your sins are like scarlet,
> They shall be as white as snow;
> Though they are red like crimson,
> They shall be as wool.
> —Isaiah 1:18

Where have you been lost? Wounded? Where have you abused your femininity, turned tricks to get what you wanted or to please others? Turning tricks may look like trying to make people love you, trying to secure affection and love and safety by acting, looking, or speaking a certain way. Perhaps you work harder, denying your own legitimate needs, in order to earn others' approval.

Krissy just wanted attention. Growing up with a bunch of foster siblings, attention from her parents was scarcer than privacy. So when puberty hit, she started sneaking off with boys from school. Their focus made her feel desirable.

Nadia became who her husband wanted her to be. She turned herself into the perfect hostess and socialite, longing to please him and to guarantee herself a place of safety. She knew about his affairs, but she loved him and didn't want to lose him.

His divorce papers signaled that it was time to heal. The masquerade party ended, and the resuscitation started. She slowly came to life through friends who cared for her, through counseling with her women's minister, and through exploring her real gifts. Now, fifteen years after the divorce, she is self-supporting and continues to grow in her relationship with God, all the while eagerly extending hospitality to others. She says, "I want them to know that with the Lord, women don't have to just survive. They can learn to live again."

At Home in the Heart of God

Like Rahab, we also can find a new home. We can find a new heart, can find the forgiveness we need, the love we crave. We can learn to live again.

Rahab, however, had to choose to find that home. She had to choose to accept the Israelites' hospitality: first, when they allowed her to dwell just outside their camp, and then when they invited her into their families. She had to learn to live without the isolation of shame, to receive the forgiveness God offered and His people extended. She chose to leave her living death, to move into a new place spiritually, emotionally, physically, rather than hold on to shame and hardness resulting from her former prostitution. She chose healing, chose to believe that she was forgiven. These are difficult choices, for to choose to receive forgiveness we must also choose to forgive those who have hurt us.

> *To forgive another who wounds you is to say, "Your actions hurt me, but no longer bind me. And I will no longer bind us with my unforgiveness. In forgiving you, I set us both free."*

What is your choice? To haul death around with you, lugging the corpse of your past and the decay of your unforgiveness and the sin others have thrown at you? Before rigor mortis sets in, before you turn into a stiff skeleton of unforgiveness and shame, take a gentle inventory.

When someone hurts you physically, sexually, the wound is much deeper than a surface scar. Your very femininity and the beauty of your heart are damaged. To forgive the abuser doesn't mean that you are saying, "It's okay, no big deal." It doesn't minimize the pain inflicted, the destruction wreaked. To forgive another who wounds you is to say, "Your actions hurt me, but they no longer bind me. And I will no longer bind us with my unforgiveness. In forgiving you, I set myself and you free."

Examine the deepest longing of your heart. How do your actions, your reactions, your relationships, your addictions relate to that longing? Our often-unnoticed and ignored longing can lead us to sell our souls: like Rahab, in many ways we seek to be noticed, loved, cared for in unhealthy ways. To make up for wounds of the past, to try to fill the bottomless pit of our abandonment needs, we find people who will promise to love us but will inevitably hurt us.[16]

This is the nature of life in a broken world.

This is why Rahab's story of hospitality is recorded in the "Hall of Faith" in Hebrews 11. In spite of—perhaps because of—her deep woundedness, she became like Christ. She extended protection over the Israelite spies.

They extended protection over her.

And because they honored their promise to save her and her family, they also honored God. Through her, God extended protection to all of us through her great-great-great-great grandson, Jesus Christ.

God is never too busy to redeem a past. He took Rahab's life, forgave her, and placed her into the lineage of Christ. A harlot!

Regardless of how many times you have abandoned your hopes
    and dreams,
regardless of how you compensated for not feeling loved,
regardless of how you acted out your woundedness,
regardless of the sin in your past,
God has room for you in His heart, in His family, and in His
    camp.

Maybe your Jordan River is just that: a plain flooded with pain, with regret, with selling out to gain love. Let God's love extend over you; let Him extend the same protection He gave to Rahab. Let God create passage into the new land, the Land of Promise, the land of redemption. Let God buy back your past and create a new future.

That is hospitality. That is our gracious, hospitable God.

So go ahead. Tie the scarlet rope in your window. God will come and rescue you.

Travel Mercies

1. When has someone offered you a safe place? What was that like for you?

2. Where have you been lost? Wounded? Where have you abused your femininity, turned tricks to get what you wanted or to please others?

3. How can you relate to Rahab's story of selling out and then being bought back?

4. What is your forgiveness journey like? Where do you sense the need to forgive? What holds you back from forgiving or from seeking forgiveness?

5. Where do you need to experience God's hospitality? How can you extend that hospitality, that grace and rescue, to others?

What Mean These Stones?

When have you experienced God's profound forgiveness? How can you craft that story for your family and friends, sharing the miracle of being included in the lineage of Jesus Christ?

Power Up

> *How long, O Lord? Will You forget me forever?*
> *How long will You hide Your face from me?*
> *How long shall I take counsel in my soul,*
> *Having sorrow in my heart daily?*
> *How long will my enemy be exalted over me?*
>
> *But I have trusted in Your mercy;*
> *My heart shall rejoice in Your salvation.*
> *I will sing to the Lord,*
> *Because He has dealt bountifully with me.*
> —*Psalm 13:1–2, 5–6*

Rock-Hard Truth

"Even in our deepest wounds
We want someone to remember,
Regardless of how hard we try to forget,

We want someone to see,
To care, to love us,
Regardless of all the *ways* we try to forget
God will not forget us.
He sees our pain
He remembers our past
He longs to tie a scarlet cord
In the window of our walled city
And rescue us."

—Jane Rubietta[17]

Remember Me, O Lord

Dear Lord,
Thank You that You do not cast stones
but rather instruct me to build stone
memorials
of Your work in my life.
Though I deserve death
Your scarlet cord of remembering
in Christ Jesus
guarantees my salvation.
Help me to walk in the forgiveness
of that love.
Use me as part of the lineage
of Jesus.
In His name.
Amen.

Memory Stone

*"Blessed be the Lord,
who has given rest to His people Israel,
according to all that He promised.
There has not failed one word
of all His good promise,
which He promised through His servant Moses."*

— *1 Kings 8:56*

CHAPTER EIGHT

ZELOPHEHAD'S DAUGHTERS:

REMEMBERING THE PROMISES OF GOD

*S*usy's parents divorced when she was very young. The shattering of childhood peace continued with her mother's remarriages and divorces and live-in boyfriends. Society expected this girl from such a broken family to fail: to end up on the street, or in jail, or as an unwed mother.

But God had other plans for her, keeping her innocent and unaware of the riskiness of her childhood, until at thirteen she accepted the life-saving gift of a relationship with Christ. At church camp when she was fifteen, she actually had not even thought about what life was like without a father. As the campers and counselors gathered for prayer for those who did not know Him, she began to weep. Her tears flowed unheeded down her cheeks, though she had no words to describe the source of her anguish.

Her youth pastor moved to her side, and spoke God's words of healing over her unrecognized wound: "The Lord God will be your Father."

Because of her emotional and even physical orphan-
ing, Susy became heavily dependent on God. "The or-
phaning became a gift; I learned over and over that I
could trust God when others would turn away."

Rather than become a victim of her circumstances,
her environment, her society, Susy made a choice as a
child of God: she moved fully into His family. People at
church poured their lives into her, opened their hearts
and homes to her; and they continue to pray for her
today. Her youth pastor's intervention, in particular,
likely saved Susy years of dysfunction, keeping her from
turning in the wrong direction.

In her orphaned state, Susy says, "God has never for-
gotten me. I have a lot of stones."

A Sibling Assembly

Five daughters. A winsome collection of women with a variety
of personalities, these daughters of Zelophehad appear on the scene
with a rare expression of assertiveness and faithfulness in the days of
Moses and Joshua.

Like Susy in our opening illustration, they are orphans of the
wilderness, these five girls. Evidently, years earlier, when first gaz-
ing at the Promised Land from the vantage point of the desert, their
father was among the Israelites who worried that God might not, after all, be a good God who kept His promises. Maybe the Promised
Land wasn't such a deal, since the spies returned from their reconnaissance mission spouting off about giants in the land and reeking
of terror at the prospect of moving by faith into a land occupied by
formidable enemies.

In fact, they wailed, "Our wives and our little ones will become
plunder; would it not be better for us to return to Egypt?" (Numbers
14:3 NASB). So they set about finding a leader to deliver them back

into the land of slavery, the very land God had just totally annihilated with plagues.

Because of their lack of faith, God said, "Your corpses shall fall in this wilderness . . . according to your complete number from twenty years old and upward, who have grumbled against Me" (Numbers 14:29 NASB).

"Your children, however, whom you said would become a prey—I will bring them in, and they shall know the land which you have rejected" (Numbers 14:31 NASB).

They buried their father in the desert, but Zelophehad's daughters survive life in the wilderness. Even so, they have reservations when they gather among the Hebrew nation, listening from the desert side of the Jordan as Moses doles out the portions of land for each tribe. The rules are clear: land will belong to the principal male in each family; if not a son, then a brother of the principal; and if not a brother, then next of kin.

The problem in this instance is that no one in Zelophehad's family seemed to have any Y chromosomes; absolutely no men exist to inherit the land being passed down through this particular grandson of Manasseh. Which means that the land would have to be given to another family, thus obliterating Zelophehad's family name from the Hebrew lineage.

$\mathcal{N}$o Land, No Life

What might this imply for the five unmarried sisters, the only surviving offspring of this family? While this doesn't seem like a big deal in our era—we can pick up the classifieds and rent an apartment with only a month's deposit and some credit references—in that time owning land meant survival. Women without property through the men in their family were not only likely homeless, but they would also have to secure themselves to a landowner elsewhere, either as hired hands, itinerant workers, or indentured servants. It also meant that women would not be apt to find a mate, because the women would be unable to offer a dowry to the prospective groom's family.

But the news gets worse. Indentured female servants also were purchased with the expectation that they would have sex with the landowner, should he so desire. Any children of the sexual union would belong to him and could be bought, sold, or sent away.

These possibilities are ominous. Add to them the fact that Zelophehad's daughters have camped for many years under the baking sun and freezing nights. Undoubtedly they are more than ready to exchange the nomadic existence of tents and sand under the flaps for real walls and a roof.

We always have a desert-side choice: stand in terror or move forward in faith.

One thing I love about this relatively obscure story in Numbers 27 and 36, and Joshua 17, is that the sisters are all named, and the action they take challenges me to take my own future in hand when necessary. They are not just "Zelophehad's girls." Mahlah, Noah, Hoglah, Milcah, and Tirzah are among the few women mentioned as daughters by name in the Scriptures.

And they leave a powerful legacy for us. Unlike their father, who looked from the desert side of the river and quailed in terror, they look from the desert side of the Jordan at flood stage and choose to forge frontward. He looked backward to Egypt; they look forward to the Land of Promise. We too always have a desert-side choice: stand in terror or move forward in faith.

These sisters have foresight, are united in purpose, move ahead courageously, and do not hesitate to stand without compromise on the promises of God.

Foresight

These women do not bury their heads in the desert sand. They are savvy products of the desert, of sun and sand and rootlessness.

Well they can imagine the benefits of owning land, and little do they want to continue life rootless, without a home, without any holdings, enslaved yet again to labor for daily bread at the hands of a slave owner.

Before they even cross the Jordan River, before the Lord commissioned Joshua to lead the people across on dry ground, the sisters look ahead. They take a good gaze at the future, and the future indeed does not look promising for orphaned girls with no principal male in the entire family. They weigh their options: indentured servitude, homelessness, no wedding bells, no *huppah*. Or, imagine! They can confront the system.

Many women would have capitulated to the structure in place. But not these women. Inherently, they must know their own value. Their own family name contributes to the community in general, to the history of their people, and to the value and richness of their nation. God selected every single person, every family, always tracing them back to their great-great-great-granddaddy, one of Jacob's twelve sons. Each person mattered to God then, and matters to God now.

Further, speaking of value, God had gone to considerable trouble to set the Hebrew people free from slavery in Egypt. The sisters cannot forget the stories of the plagues, the race through the desert to the Red Sea, and God's mighty breath blowing a dry path for them to cross over. How, then, can a future as indentured servants possibly appeal to these five women? Indeed, to God?

*U*nited in Purpose

Maybe they griped and complained when they first met together —who would blame them? Isn't that part of Roberta's Rules of Order: every meeting must begin with whining and wailing! But ultimately the five sisters bring the meeting to purpose: "What will we do about our future?"

In this instance, they live up to their father's name, which means "to unify." They know they are stronger together. Individual power and purpose are far less important and more impotent than people gathered together in common purpose. We are much stronger united in community rather than isolated in our individual pursuits.

ℬelonging, not belongings, indicates our worth.

So together the sisters decide about their inheritance. And isn't inheritance the cause of many a family feud? How many siblings have not spoken to one another since the reading of a family member's last will and testament? "I wanted the antique table and you got it. . . . Daddy always said I could have his desk, not you. . . . Momma loved me best and that's why I got the ring and you didn't." Whether we voice these words or not, too often the possessions we fight over take precedence over the people in our lives. We weigh our worth by our belongings, rather than by the only sound measuring device: God's love for us.

"God *so loved* the world that He gave His only begottenSon, that whosoever believes in Him should not perish but have everlasting life" (John 3:16, emphasis mine). That clears away all the smoke and fog created by worries about worth. Belonging is everything if we want to live well. Belonging, not belongings, indicates our worth.

Belonging—to one another and to God—will take this family into their future. Mahlah, Noah, Hoglah, Milcah, and Tirzah decide that staying together requires standing together. They draw on their family name "to unify," and link arms to walk strongly across their Jordan River into their future—a future that only their conviction, courage, and God's heart can create.

*C*ourageous Movement

These are uncharted waters—or sand dunes. No woman had ever had to take a stand for her future, calling for her rights in such a way before, because no one had even owned land in recent Hebrew history, as in the past four-hundred-plus years. And prior to Joseph settling in Egypt with his family, from the time of Abraham their forefathers and foremothers had lived as nomads, always following God's leading, touring about with their camels and caravans and all their worldly goods, always en route to the promise of God: "Now look toward the heavens, and count the stars, if you are able to count them. . . . So shall your descendants be" (Genesis 15:5 NASB). The book of Hebrews tells us, "By faith [Abraham] lived as an alien in the land of promise, as in a foreign land, dwelling in tents with Isaac and Jacob" (11:9 NASB).

Up until the time of Zelophehad's daughters, their lives were portable: shake 'em out, roll 'em up, move 'em out.

Because of the precedent, it would be easier for the daughters to fold their hands and lower their eyes and follow the leader, rather than assert themselves. How often have you known that a situation required action, but not had the energy or willpower or strength to act on that need?

So many times I have passively waited for someone else to do something, hoping of course that they would magically know exactly what I wanted without my saying anything, and often without my even knowing what I wanted in the first place.

Sometimes, at home and at work, we confuse godly submission with not communicating our wants and needs, or our gifts and talents. First Peter 3:7 tells husbands, "Dwell with them with understanding, giving honor to the wife." But husbands can't understand us if we don't talk to them!

And at work: what if, during workplace evaluations, the manager invites open discussion about strengths and weaknesses, and then works to put employees in the places where they best fit? We need an open-door policy if we are going to be a good team, and that requires communicating. This is true in any relationship: marriage, family, work, friendship, volunteering.

We can't expect anyone to read our minds except God! And even though God obviously knows what's in our hearts and minds—remember Psalm 139:2–4: "I'm an open book to you; even from a distance, you know what I'm thinking. . . . You know everything I'm going to say before I start the first sentence" (THE MESSAGE)—God often waits for us to know our own hearts, to be still long enough to listen, and then to ask Him for help. Doesn't James 4:2 say exactly that? "Yet you do not have because you do not ask."

*God waits for us to know our own
hearts, to be still long enough to listen,
and then to ask Him for help.*

Undoubtedly, these women had to confront their fears: "We don't want to be indentured servants. We don't want to be homeless. We don't want to be forced into a compromising situation with a landowner."

And surely they also had to acknowledge their desires: "We want to have a home. We want to have husbands. We want to bear children. We want to be part of the settling of Israel. We want to get out of this tent!"

And then they had to move forward. Enough planning and plotting. They had to take their legitimate plea to the person in charge, even if he was the biggest man on campus: Moses.

The Scriptures tell us, "Then the daughters of Zelophehad . . . came near. . . . They stood before Moses and before Eleazar the priest and before the leaders and all the congregation at the doorway of the tent of meeting" (Numbers 27:1–2 NASB).

What women! I want to be like them when I grow up. They didn't waste time grumbling about the unfairness of their plight. They shook the sand from their skirts and headed for the powers that be. Imagine standing before Moses, the mightiest leader of all time, the human head of their nation, the one who spoke with God face-to-face. Put yourself in their sandals as they rooted themselves before him, the priest, the congregational leaders, and all their peers.

Yet we see no record of their fear. Only of their courage. With eloquence, they present their case to Moses and the rest of the nation.

*H*onoring the Name

These five sisters are not just trying to seize a future for themselves. They also don't want their father's name to pass out of the
history of Israel; they want to keep his good name and to honor it.
His name represented his identity and reputation, creating a standard
for his children to live up to. "A good name is better than precious
ointment" (Ecclessiastes 7:1).

Pushing their way to the front of the crowd, the women unite
before Moses: "Our father died in the wilderness . . . and he had no
sons. Why should the name of our father be withdrawn from among
his family because he had no son? Give us a possession among our
father's brothers" (Numbers 27:3 NASB).

I like it that they honored their father's name, and in doing so,
set a system in place for their own future. When I grew up, my own
father traveled a great deal with his work, and I was one of eight children. My mother's plate was full to overflowing! Yet she did not
speak badly against my dad; and when times were hard, which they
frequently were, she moved resolutely forward, accomplishing each
task and caring for us well, saying it was all "for the Lord's name's
sake." She determined to honor her heavenly Father as well as my
earthly father.

We can never go wrong if we refuse to bad-mouth our family of
origin. This doesn't mean that you gloss over your past, pretending
that you had a perfect childhood and perfect parents and a plush, perfect pattern for moving onward.

Two sisters came to Jane at a women's retreat. Though broken
by their childhood, God rescued them and began a mighty healing
work. Still, the specter of their parents' failure haunted them. Daily
they asked, "Why did they act like that? Why would they hurt us
so?" Though it isn't always the case, the truth that began to finally
set them free was this: Most parents do the best they can for their
children. Often they act out of their own brokenness or lack of
knowledge, but in many situations are powerless to act differently
until God begins a resuscitation in their hearts. Honoring our family
means standing up for the very best in them and for them, and refusing to bow to the bondage of bitterness.

Zelophehad's daughters didn't deny their father's sin. In fact, they said, "Our father died in the wilderness . . . in his own sin" (Numbers 27:3). And that's the truth for all of us: our parents are sinners. We are sinners. We are all broken by our separation from God, and this brokenness will show up in our lives, before we know Christ and after we have claimed His saving name as our own. It will impact those we love, though we wish it otherwise.

Remembering can lead you to either regress or progress. The choice is yours!

This too is part of the grace of honoring the name: If our sin didn't show up, then we would continue to pretend: that Christianity is some magical formula; that faith in God means no problems; don't worry, be happy. But thanks be to God! Like the old hymn says, "Grace, grace, God's grace, grace that is greater than all our sins . . ." God's goodness and love don't eradicate your past or your present sins and wounds, but rather heal them, allowing you to move forward into your future as the woman He created you to be.

Remembering can lead you to either regress or progress. The choice is yours! These sisters looked back, with honesty and integrity, and then moved forward, stepping firmly on God's Word. They were ready to leave behind the stigma of Egypt. Ready to claim their promise as children of God, redeemed, saved from slavery, set free to live in the land flowing with milk and honey.

Standing on the Promises

A good leader is not afraid to ask for help, for clarification, for wisdom; and Moses is one of the best leaders of all time. When the sisters bring the problem of inheritance to him, Moses—who has not encountered this issue—takes it to God, seeking His Word.

And God's answer resounds clearly:

"The daughters of Zelophehad speak what is right; you shall surely give them a possession of inheritance among their father's brothers, and cause the inheritance of their father to pass to them. And you shall speak to the children of Israel, saying: 'If a man dies and has no son, then you shall cause his inheritance to pass to his daughter. If he has no daughter, then you shall give his inheritance to his brothers. If he has no brothers, then you shall give his inheritance to his father's brothers.'" (Numbers 27:7–10)

Beautiful, isn't it? God was counting on these daughters in order to establish His will in Israel! They move forward in faith, after listening to their hearts, and so step right into God's plan for their lives.

This is true for you as well: God counts on you to establish His will in your life and in the lives of those you love. Listen to your heart, seek God's wisdom, move forward in faith, and step into God's plan for your life.

*O*n the Other Side

Once across the Jordan, after conquering the most obvious local enemies, Joshua begins the task of settling the several million Israelites and all their belongings. Calling on the system in place through Moses, he parcels out land packages.

When Joshua reaches the family of Manasseh, the sisters step forward, again united in purpose and intent to honor their father's name. Even more than that, they step forward and stand firmly on the words of God, spoken on the other side of the river, to Moses and all the people. They remember aloud:

"The Lord commanded Moses to give us an inheritance among our brothers" (Joshua 17:4). Hear that? "The Lord commanded." This is the ultimate stance and standard: God's Word, God's commandment. They pull on God's trustworthy, inviolable Word. They recite His command and claim their inheritance.

God's Word in response brooks no argument: "Therefore, according to the commandment of the Lord, he gave them an inheritance among their father's brothers. Ten shares fell to Manasseh . . .

because the daughters of Manasseh received an inheritance among his sons" (Joshua 17:4–6).

So go ahead. Keep hiding God's Word in your heart and then call on that Scripture. Quote it daily. Take the Lord at His Word even when it doesn't make sense. Stand on what is right, on what God says.

*O*rphans of the Wilderness

The story of the daughters of Zelophehad begins with their fatherlessness: "Our father died . . ." They are orphans of the wilderness. And throughout the pages of Scriptures, God's heart for the fatherless appears again and again. He promises to provide for them in the Land of Promise. He will take care of them, their needs, their hopes, their fears, their futures.

Perhaps you are a literal orphan as well. Or maybe you are an emotional orphan or widow, never receiving the love you deserved and longed for from your parents, siblings, or husband. Maybe life's floodplains swept away your husband or parents or best friend: They left you physically because they simply could not navigate their own floods and tend to your needs as well, or they encountered wounds they could not stitch closed. Perhaps you are married but do not have a spiritual or emotional helpmate, someone to stand by your side.

In the midst of emotional, spiritual, or physical orphaning, be careful how you choose to meet those very legitimate and God-given needs. It is easy to look in all the wrong places for someone to fill the wounds left by others.

Abby's mother had been emotionally distant from her, and Abby never felt good enough, pretty enough, smart enough. Abby adored her father, a kind man who worked long hours, and was absent physically from his daughter's life. In college, Abby turned to a friend who preyed upon her neediness and took her under her wing, then seduced her into a same-sex relationship.

Yvette didn't notice her own orphaned heart until she ended up married with two children and a workaholic husband. Her marriage crumbled, and she landed in counseling. Finally, there she unearthed the broken pieces of her childhood, which continued to wound her in her marriage. There she wrestled with the choices she'd made, bad choices, but choices that stemmed from her longing to be cared for and protected. And there she began, finally, to trust God to be her provider, to parent her as her own parents were unable to do.

Invite the family of God to surround you if you have been orphaned by desert storms, by sin in the wilderness, by flooding rivers, and fallible human beings. The Lord commands us to "Rejoice with those who rejoice, and weep with those who weep" (Romans 12:15), and tells us that, "Pure and undefiled religion before God and the Father is this: to visit orphans and widows in their trouble, and to keep oneself unspotted from the world" (James 1:27). When you invite others into your heart, you are asking them, as the daughters of Zelophehad asked, to remember God's promises, to remember that, "the Lord commanded. . . ."

Even though you may feel alone, you are not alone. Not only will Christ never leave you or forsake you, but Hebrews 12:22 says that you are in "an innumerable company of angels." I remember one time at home, literally sensing the presence and protective covering of God over me. I actually felt the impression of someone hovering over me and stopped to thank God for His angels.

There is no shame in an orphaned or abandoned state. But please choose not to remain there. Can you see your current state as a gift? When you recognize abandonment, move into the mentality of needing the Lord. You can deliberately step into your rightful position as a child of your heavenly Father. Your heart can beat in rhythm, "Don't forget me, Lord." Look to God and to God's people to form a network under and around you, to help you cross over the Jordan River. Hold fast, and cross over into your rightful inheritance as a child of God, a child of the Father who longs to comfort you and help you to walk into the promises stored up for you.

Seeing God's Glory

When you stand at the Jordan River, wondering whether to regress or progress, remember. Remember how the Israelites saw

God's glory and His miraculous signs all the way from Egypt to the edge of the Promised Land. Remember that they still did not believe Him. Imagine: seeing the glory of the Lord and not believing that if He'd rescued you once, He could do it again and again and again (Numbers 14:22–23). And yet they turned from the Promised Land and vowed to return to slavery.

Rather than trust the promises of the God who'd delivered them from slavery with such a mighty, outstretched arm, the people of Israel wanted to retreat to Egypt. From my vantage point, with a Bible at hand and knowing the facts of God's rescues and the certain future for His people, their fear seems ridiculous.

But in truth, they stared at the unknown future and simply forgot the Lord's faithfulness, forgot about His might, forgot about His goodness stored up for them, forgot about His promise.

Don't forget! Don't forget God's glory, the ways He has guided you in the past up to this very intersection of fear and faith. Don't forget to remember God's longing—His promise to bring you too — just like the daughters of Zelophehad, into the land flowing with milk and honey, into your rightful inheritance. Stand on that promise, and then, like a bride, let your Bridegroom who will never leave you nor forsake you lift you in His arms and carry you across the river.

Travel Mercies

1. When have you faced a desert-side choice to stand in terror or forge forward in faith? What were the temptations to "return to Egypt"? What was the Land of Promise? How did you ultimately respond?

2. When have you known that a situation required action but not had the energy or willpower to act? When have you relied on the past—"We've never done it that way before"—rather than look to the future? What role models of passivity, however loving these people may be, fill your past or present? How will you learn to listen to your heart and take your heart to God?

3. Where would you like to airbrush your past? How can you be honest about your past, and even your present imperfections, and still honor your family name?

4. When have you felt orphaned or widowed? How have you tried to cover that pain in unhealthy ways? What will it look like to lean on God's parenting and His promise, "I will never desert you, nor will I ever forsake you" (Hebrews 13:5 NASB)? Where is your network in the body of Christ?

5. Where have you seen God's glory? The cloud by day, the fire by night? When has remembering God's glory helped you to stand firm and move ahead?

What Mean These Stones?

Consider these words: "You know in all your hearts and in all your souls that not one word of all the good words which the Lord your God spoke concerning you has failed; all have been fulfilled for you, not one of them has failed" (Joshua 23:14 NASB).

Look at your flooding river. Now choose one of God's promises. (There are a million of them!) Hold onto it, hide it in your heart, and then use it as a shield about you to move forward.

Power Up

> "In your unfailing love
> you will lead the people
> you have redeemed.
> In your strength You will guide them
> to your holy dwelling. . . .
> You will bring them in
> and plant them on the mountain
> of your inheritance—

the place, O LORD,
you made for your dwelling,
the sanctuary, O LORD,
your hands established.
The LORD will reign
for ever and ever."
  —*Exodus* 15:13, 17–18 *NIV*

Rock-Hard Truth

"Our longing desires can no more exhaust the fullness of the treasures of the Godhead, than our imagination can touch their measure. . . . Every gift of God is but a harbinger of His greatest and only sufficing gift—that of Himself. No gift unrecognized as coming from God is at its own best; therefore many things that God would gladly give us, things even that we need because we are, must wait until we ask for them, that we may know whence they come: when in all gifts we find Him, then in Him we shall find all things."
  —George MacDonald, *Unspoken Sermons*[18]

Remember Me, O Lord

Father God,
Thank You that Your arms are strong and Your promises true.
Thank You that You long to bring me into Your heart,
into Your home, into Your Promised Land.
Thank You for the deep waters of my past:
the pain, the promises, the brokenness, the goodness.
Thank You that even these can bring You honor.

Help me to honor my family name,
by choosing healing for my past,
by choosing to believe the best about my family,
by choosing to move forward
across the Jordan River
to become the woman of Your dreams.
In Jesus' name.
Amen.

Memory Stone

"The Lord bless you and keep you;
The Lord make His face shine upon you,
And be gracious to you;
The Lord lift up His countenance upon you,
And give you peace."

— Numbers 6:24-26

CHAPTER NINE

ACHSAH:

REMEMBERING THE BLESSING OF GOD

Esther yanked the photo album off the coffee table, then raced to the bookshelf for the rest of her collection. Thirty-five years of marriage. What a waste. She flipped open the first album and ripped a photo of her husband off the page, tearing it in half with immense satisfaction. There, a picture of the two of them! Shredded. Aha—that trip to the water-fall. Rip. Oh, look. Dick holding their first puppy. Grrrr. Gone.

The pieces of pictures, remnants of their life together, piled up around Esther. But still she kept at it. How dare he smile at her in that way in that picture? Forget how nice his eyes were. Rip.

But her hands slowed, and she gazed at the man she married. There he was, helping the neighbor with his car. And there, with the children—what a good dad he'd been to their kids. He'd wrestle with them while she stood on the *side, wringing her hands and saying, "Now, Dick, that's enough. Dick, stop now." And the kids laughing and shrieking and giving as good as they got.*

Here they were on their anniversary. He'd actually managed to bring her flowers that day. And there was their first home they'd purchased. Remember how he carried her over the threshold, hugging her tight in a newlywed-like grip, and how they'd ended up on the floor in their empty bedroom . . . ?

And remember . . .

And remember . . .

Before long, tears rivered down Esther's cheeks, and her hands stilled over the ripping and shredding. He was a good man. He loved her, even though sometimes he didn't love her the way she wanted to be loved.

And there, over the photo albums, she fell in love with her husband again, the man she married, the man who frustrated the life out of her, and the only man who'd ever made her laugh deep belly-laughs.

She swept up the photo bits and slid them into an envelope, a memento of what she'd almost lost. A reminder of how vital it is to release the hard times and to remember the blessings of their relationship.

A Trophy Bride

Meet Achsah, another bride in another era. She has been raised by a strong-minded man, a warrior, a man of deep faith and powerful action. Her daddy's name, Caleb, means *forceful*, and forceful he was. He knew right from wrong and acted on the right, even when the majority opinion was against him. He was one of two men who stood up to all of Israel when they wanted to flee from the Promised Land on the first spying trip.

It is no surprise, then, that Caleb's daughter Achsah appears on the scene in a display of wisdom and strength. We find this rare woman in Joshua 15:16–19: She knows her own mind, knows what she needs, and has the courage to ask for it.

When the Israelites move into the Promised Land, Joshua details the passing out of inheritance to each tribe and family. After receiving his allotment, Caleb posts a reward: "The one who attacks Kiriath-sepher and captures it, I will give him Achsah my daughter as a wife" (Joshua 15:16 NASB).

Settling down is undoubtedly a high motivation for the travel-weary soldiers, to say nothing of marrying into the family of a mighty war hero and leader. Othniel rises to the challenge, capturing the village and winning himself a bride.

His new wife, Achsah, immediately ascertains the importance of owning land—perhaps she is friends with Zelophehad's girls!—and "persuaded him to ask her father for a field" (Joshua 15:18). Caleb awards them the land of the Negev, semi-arid territory south of Judea.

She surveys their holdings and realizes another necessity: No one can farm without a source of freshwater on the land. So off she trots on her donkey. Finding her father, she slides from the donkey and says, "Give me a blessing; since you have given me the land of the Negev, give me also springs of water" (v. 19 NASB).

Caleb responds to her need by giving her the upper springs and the lower springs, a substantial gift to his forthright daughter. It speaks volumes of his love for her and his desire to see her well-settled.

Bringing Out the Best

A good relationship brings out the best in each individual, and surely this is true of the marriage between Achsah and her warrior. Not only does Othniel capture the city to win her hand, and follow his wife's wisdom about land, he also demonstrates the truth of his name, "force of God," by living it out.

After the Israelites settle into their new territory, Joshua, Caleb, and the other leaders who bore witness to God's mighty acts die. Within the span of one generation, "the sons of Israel did what was evil in the sight of the Lord, and forgot the Lord their God" (Judges 3:7 NASB). To combat the evil, God appoints Othniel, Achsah's husband, as a judge over the nation. Bringing order out of absolute chaos and debauchery, he rules for forty years. He is a force of God amongst a nation swept under the current of sin and idolatry.

Good relationships call out the strengths in both people.

Good relationships call out the strengths in both people. Whether a married couple or friends (or both!) or colleagues, they challenge one another to use the gifts they have received. With a love that is unconditional, a love that says, "I will love you even if you fail," they beckon one another to growth. Real love, Christ-like love, seeks the best for the other person.

This is true at work too. Sometimes we may see an employee underfunctioning or underperforming. Rather than release the person from the job, instead we try to listen to the other's giftings and strengths. We try to clarify our visions and then move them within those boundaries. We strengthen the movement of the whole by putting the individual in the right place.

Ellen is a painter now—but she'd never thought about watercolor until her husband bought her a beautiful painting set for her birthday. His love invited her to experiment with a medium she hadn't considered. She says, "John's paint set gift nudged me gently into an unexplored area of my life, and eventually exposed a spiritual gift for creativity. I never, ever was encouraged to draw, paint, create art by anyone in my life until I received that set. As I take stock of the art I've created in the past twenty years, it's amazing to realize that none of it may have been if my husband hadn't gently challenged me. And the bigger tragedy would have been not having a creative outlet, spiritually, emotionally, relationally."

Ellen, in turn, gifted John with her belief in him. When fascination with all things related to computers blended with his expertise with sound, she backed him as he began to discover new ways to transmit sound over the Internet. She says, "What a privilege to support his dreams."

Their love for one another gave them permission to grow.

$\mathcal{R}$emembering

Based on a true story, the movie *Cinderella Man* features a boxer during the Great Depression, a champion from the 1920s who lost his spark of genius in the ring. Food lines and public assistance deepened his despair. He hit bottom when the electric company disconnected his electricity, and his wife placed their children in a warmer home until the situation improved.

James J. Braddock decided to give the ring one more left-right punch when his former manager, Joe, offered a final fight possibility: come out of decommissioned status and fight in the preliminary round for World Heavyweight Champion. The underdog, James won the fight and went on to the World Championship.

$\mathcal{R}$ecalling past victories fuels us,
moving us forward into victory.

Before this fight, as in previous fights, Joe began a locker-room litany to James: "Who beat that John Henry Lewis?" *"Jim Braddock."* "Who whopped that Art Lasky punk?" *"James J. Braddock."* Before long, James smiled as his manager recounted victories in the past, empowering and encouraging him toward victory in the next fight.

Just so, we move from victory to victory. Recalling past victories fuels us, moving us forward into victory for our next battle. When Caleb gave Achsah and her husband the territory in the south, he gave her a portion of land rich in history, where walking the arid hills called up memories. Here Abraham, their forefather, first moved with his wife, his brother Lot, and their immense properties (Genesis 13:1). Here Hagar fled when her mistress Sarah, Abraham's wife, treated her badly. Here an angel met Hagar and tended to her needs (Genesis 16:7, 14). Here Isaac and Jacob lived (Genesis 24:62; 37:1).

Here was the land that Caleb and Joshua spied out nearly four decades previously (Numbers 13:22), the land where the enemies were big but their God even bigger.

Do these stories of faith, these tales of God's leading and provision, ruminate in Achsah's mind as she walks the territory her father gave to her and her groom? Surely her people recount God's faithfulness as they settle into the Negev. Surely these rich historical vignettes become bedtime stories to share with her own children as she hands down to them a heritage of faith. Surely when the time comes for hard decisions, faith-filled decisions, the very sand on which Achsah stands reminds her to choose the right path, the narrow way, as difficult as it might be.

Choosing the Best

Achsah has little choice in her marriage mate. Parents arranged the weddings and the children simply fell in place, assuming that their parents knew best. Love wasn't an issue.

Achsah brings her best self and her gifts to the relationship.

Achsah could enter into this covenant like a martyr, dragging her feet into the relationship and minimizing herself. She could steep her soul in the vinegar of spite and resentment. She could passively wait for her new husband to make all the decisions and help her feel good about herself while she just keeps her mouth shut, refusing to create love in their marriage. She could choose to put her own mind and heart on hold, icing them over, slowly dying in a relationship where she has no choice.

But she doesn't. She brings her best self and her gifts to the relationship.

What situations are you in where you feel you have no say, no choice? Where your reflex is to sit back and hope that something changes? To cry out, "Woe is me" and throw yourself a pity party? Maybe it's your marriage, like Esther in our opening example. Your husband still doesn't bring you flowers. He doesn't romance you. He doesn't provide for you very well financially and certainly not emotionally.

Or maybe it's your job. You hate your job, but what can you do? You have to work. So you plod to work, doing the bare minimum, punching in, punching out. Or you hate your course work so you complain and moan through each credit hour.

How can you choose the best in places that are less than ideal? What would it look like for you to bring your best self to your job? Your marriage? To choose to bring out the best in the people around you, whether it's your home or your workplace or your church? How could you begin to discern, verbalize, and act on your own needs, hopes, dreams?

Knowing Your Needs

What creates the ability to ask for what you need? Achsah knew she needed land, and when she saw the land, knew she needed water on it.

If you were to compose a list of your needs, what would that list include? How can you use your gifts to begin meeting those needs and getting around the obstacles without destroying your relationships along the way? Without moving to the polar opposite, a life of self-centered focus?

When trying to figure out God's will and her own needs and goals, our friend Ruthie says, "God can direct our paths better when our feet are moving." She tries to follow God's known will for her as found in Scripture, the places where the Lord is very clear about what He wants in His kids. "You shall love the Lord your God with all your heart, and with all your soul, and with all your mind, and with all your strength. . . . You shall love your neighbor as yourself" (Mark 12:30–31 NASB).

And as she seeks God's heart, releasing her desires into His caring and capable hands, she finds her next step on the path is made clear. She doesn't wait for a magical revelation to spring forth, like piped-in Muzak: "I want you to do this, Ruthie." She knows what He wants in terms of her heart, and she gives Him her attention and keeps moving so He can direct her path. She tries to listen to her longings, to access her gifts and passions, and then commits herself to obedience. Even if it means some sand in her shoes. As she moves forward, God moves as well. Just like the ten lepers seeking healing: Jesus said to them, "Go and show yourselves to the priests." And as they moved in obedience, they were healed (Luke 17:11–14 NASB).

*L*iving in a Dry Land

Achsah's inheritance isn't ideal. This isn't the tropics, a rainforest redolent with exotic flowers and spicy herbs, with lush growth and waterfalls. This is very close to the desert, with sand and dry air, cold nights and hot days.

*L ist the positives
in your negative situation.*

But does she waste time whining about what she doesn't have? Perhaps in the quiet of her bedroom sometimes, she does. But in the light of day, she determines what it will take to live well in that dry place. She knows enough about desert living to know that deserts can bloom with the proper irrigation, and clearly formulates and verbalizes her plan.

This is definitely the road less traveled for some of us.

My mother lived tucked away in the middle of nowhere for years while my father worked. I know she longed for more intimacy with him. She didn't get what she wanted or expected, but she held on to her attitude and her heart. What she did receive was far beyond anything she could have imagined: a sweet, deep relationship with her Lord.

Life is hard. But belaboring the difficulties through negative words harms us, and the Enemy uses them against us. A misconception or common deception about the scope of our Enemy's power and abilities is that he would have us believe that he knows everything we're thinking, and there is nothing we can hide from him. Our deception on that point needlessly allows him to discourage and intimidate us. Of course our thoughts aren't completely private; God Himself shows repeatedly in Scripture that He's aware of everything going on in our minds. "The Lord knows the thoughts of man" (Psalm 94:11); "All things are naked and open to the eyes of Him to whom we must give account" (Hebrews 4:13). But nowhere do the Scriptures tell us that the Devil or his demons can know our thoughts. Be very careful what comes out of your mouth, because only then can they use what comes out of your mouth to discourage you.

And keep a clean heart. One of Jackie's many stepfathers was harsh and controlling. Her uncle and mentor told her, "Do the right thing in that situation." One day, as she read her Bible, the Holy Spirit convicted Jackie of unforgiveness. The Lord brought her uncle's words back to her mind, and she apologized for her attitude. Subtle changes appeared in their relationship after that: the tension lessened and the peace increased.

Where are you living right now? In the semi-arid climate of the desert with a parched soul? How will you live well in that dry place? What would good soul care look like for you? What if you decide what fruit you would like to see God bring forth in your life, from your soul, in this place, and put that before the Lord? What if you choose how you will landscape the desert portions of your world?

And do you dare to do what Achsah does?

*A*sking for a Blessing

Achsah goes where no other woman thus far in Scripture has dared to tread: as her father's daughter, Achsah freely says, "Give me a blessing." The precedent has been for the firstborn son to receive the blessing, but rarely did he even ask for it: it was understood that he would be the one blessed, the one receiving the larger portion of the estate and the father's legacy as well as the spiritual headship of the clan.

Remember the treacherous and painful story of Jacob, asking for his father's blessing while pretending to be Esau, the firstborn son? (See vv. 18–29.) Desperate for a blessing, Jacob lived down to his name, "the deceiver," when he lied and connived in order to receive the blessing. When are you desperate for a blessing? What would you do to receive it? How does that longing show up in your actions?

*How does your longing for a blessing
show up in your actions?*

The conversation in Joshua 15:16–19 between Caleb and Achsah seems stark and bare:
"What do you wish?"
"Give me a blessing."
No beating around the bush—father and daughter very directly get to the point. Their words seem demanding, even brusque. No soft, tender hellos, how are yous, I am fines. No gentle inquiries about how the new marriage is working out, whether the traffic was bad, or the donkey ride lumpy and bumpy. We don't see hugs or kisses.

We just see straight-ahead communication with no risk of misunderstanding.

This is actually refreshing: Caleb and his daughter are clear about their relationship; they evidently respect each other and can get right to the meat of the matter.

What a good role model for us.

And yet, *blessing* is not a vocabulary word in our primary relationships. When did you last say to your best friend or sister or boyfriend or father or husband, "Give me a blessing"? Wouldn't you feel presumptuous to ask them, "How can I bless you today?" as though it would be vain to believe that you might be able to actually be, or give, a blessing?

If they asked *you*, "Give me a blessing," how would you bless them? Would you stumble over your words and falter around, never having thought about your heart's deepest hopes for them?

Blessing is an awkward business: it either appears greedy or vain, the opposite of humility. And God? How dare we ask Him for a blessing? It is scandalous.

Let's clarify: We're not talking about blessing in the sense of material prosperity—stuff—the accumulation that the world judges us by, the mentality that God is blessing you if you own lots of possessions. Yes, Achsah asks her father for springs of water on their property, which is the equivalent of asking for life. This seems like something God would delight to give, just as a good earthly father would. Didn't God provide water in the wilderness for His people?

We can't measure God's blessing by the presence, or absence, of material goods or a trouble-free life. As my husband says, "God is not some cosmic Santa Claus." He wants a relationship with you, wants you to know His heart for you, wants to put His Word in you (John 15:7) and to bless others through you. That *is* the blessing.

A favorite blessing is at Jesus' baptism, when the Holy Spirit descended on Christ in the form of a dove and the voice of God flowed from heaven in a wondrous gift, "This is my beloved Son; in Him I am well-pleased." And when Jesus shared the story of the master who dispensed talents to three workers, and said to the one who invested his talent wisely, "Well done. . . . Enter into the joy of your lord" (Matthew 25:23). We crave God's "well done," His love, approval, joy—His blessing!—and we enter into God's plan for us when this is our heart's desire. For this God created us!

Hands-On Blessing

Jesus carried out the tradition of Jewish blessing when parents wanted to bring their children to Him, but the disciples tried to push them away. Jesus said, "'Let the little children come to Me, and do not forbid them; for of such is the kingdom of God. . . .' And He took them up in His arms, laid His hands on them, and blessed them" (Mark 10:13–16).

The Scriptures tell us that through Christ, God has "blessed us with every spiritual blessing in the heavenly places" (Ephesians 1:3), but we need to have that verbalized for us; we need for others to literally touch us with a gracious blessing. If you have not experienced the "localized" blessing of God through your parents, much like Jesus laid hands on the children and blessed them, don't bow to self-pity. Don't live an underpowered life either, because of the lack of blessing. Instead, invite people who know and love you to speak blessing over you. Ask an older couple, or your pastor or youth minister, to bless you. We have had a ceremony of blessing the children at our church, and know of youth groups where students and mentors gather for the specific purpose of conveying a blessing to the youth of the church. Don't allow the deficits in your past to hinder your future or to become stumbling blocks for walking well in this land called earth. We are called to walk in the heart of God's blessing.

In the context of the Old Testament, the heart of the blessing was the pronouncement that the covenant promised of God would come through that individual being blessed. The Lord says to Abraham, "I will bless you, and will make your name great; and so you shall be a blessing . . . and in you all the families of the earth shall be blessed" (Genesis 12:2–3 NASB).

Still, critics consider asking for God's blessing to be selfish, self-centered, inappropriate. Yet,

To bless in the biblical sense means to ask for or to impart supernatural favor. When we ask for God's blessing, we're not asking for more of what we could get for ourselves. We're crying out for the wonderful, unlimited goodness that only God has the power to know about or to give us. This kind of richness is what the writer was referring to in

Proverbs: "The Lord's blessing is our greatest wealth. All our work adds nothing to it!" (10:22 TLB). [Asking for a blessing] focuses on our wanting for ourselves nothing more and nothing less than what God wants for us.[19]

This strikes me as highly intelligent, rather than selfish. What if, when you pray over your children or your husband, you mean blessing in that sense: "God, help them to want nothing more and nothing less than what You want for them"? What if, when you say, "God, bless me," your heart cry is for the depth and breadth and fullness of God's love and goodness?

The rock-hard truth is that God loves you. Loves you. Loves *you.* Let that into your thirsty heart. And if life is hard right now, it doesn't diminish God's love. If your Jordan River is flooding and you do not sense God's blessing—God doesn't seem to be answering —could you say, "Father, please show me Your goodness in this rock-hard place and help me to recognize it"?

A Daddy's Gift

"Look what I brought you!" Every time Tony returned from a trip, he brought home presents for the kids. They weren't big-budget items, and the kids didn't care about their monetary worth. These gifts said to them, "I missed you. I was thinking of you. I love you."

These gifts meant so much to our children, in fact, that they looked forward to him leaving again, so he could come home with another present. His absence meant a gift was coming! As with Tony, when God seems absent from us, when it seems like God is gone, is silent, He is probably working on another part of your plan, and at the right time He will come with another gift.

A good father delights to give good gifts to his children, and of all the earthly daddies around, none compare to our heavenly Father. Jesus says in Luke 11:9–10, "So I say to you, ask, and it will be given to you; seek, and you will find; knock, and it will be opened to you. For everyone who asks, receives; and he who seeks, finds; and to him who knocks, it will be opened" (NASB).

"Uh-huh," you say. "I've been praying. Then why can't I pay my bills? Why is my husband unemployed? Why don't I have a husband? Why is my child running from God?"

Jesus' words are not a formula for a health-and-wealth type of life. Beware of measuring God's blessing by the absence of trouble or conflict in your life. Yes, perhaps you have seen the occasional good gift from your own daddy. But how can the God of all the universe feel this way about you? Doesn't all the evidence point painfully to the contrary?

Jesus follows His directive about asking, seeking, knocking with a story:

> "Don't bargain with God. Be direct. Ask for what you need. This is not a cat-and-mouse, hide-and-seek game we're in. If your little boy asks for a serving of fish, do you scare him with a live snake on his plate? If your little girl asks for an egg, do you trick her with a spider? As bad as you are, you wouldn't think of such a thing—you're at least decent to your own children. And don't you think the Father who conceived you in love will give the Holy Spirit when you ask him?" (Luke 11:11–13 THE MESSAGE)

Isn't the Holy Spirit the very fullness of God Himself, the presence and power and goodness of our Lord filling us? This is the essence of the blessing. How amazing to receive such a rich gift. And of course our heavenly Daddy, our Abba, when we ask Him for His blessing, will give us what is very best for us. We can trust that, and let Him define how that will look.

After all, when we didn't even know what we needed, didn't He give us Jesus?

𝒜 Tinkling Ornament

Achsah's name can either mean *stockade* or *anklet*, as in a tinkling ornament around one's ankle. It can mean shackles, or it can be an adornment, an enhancement.

Like our lives, there is a balance between asking for what we need

("Give me some land!") and being a beautiful addition to the lives around us. We women can easily take things too far, becoming demanding and demeaning in our rolling-tank approach to life. We hyper-control the people around us so that our world feels under control; we flatten others while we try to run our portion of the universe and theirs as well. We become like a prison guard; people see us coming and run for cover, trying to avoid life in the stocks of our choosing.

Maybe we camouflage our steamroller—maybe we sweetly go about our lives under the mask of godliness but are running the entire church by our own iron fists. Or ruling our homes. Or commandeering the committees for which we so generously volunteer our time and gifts and efforts.

But in reality, we are just trying to get our own way, trying to control the outcome and not leave anything to chance. Or to others. Or to God.

We become iron shackles, chains clattering our imprisonment, even as we do the spiritual shuffle.

How much better to be a tinkling ornament, a charming reminder of God's goodness and grace and love. When the past raises its ugly head and threatens to take over your tongue, call on God's Word. Hold on to the truth of Psalm 1, quoting Scripture and praying. Paul says in 1 Corinthians 13:1, "If I speak with the tongues of men and of angels, but do not have love, I have become a noisy gong or a clanging cymbal" (NASB).

Are you tired of being your own brass band, creating your own parade, running your own variety show? Are you weary of pounding on heaven's door with your needs, only to receive the wooden door of silence? Are your past failures controlling your movement into the future? Wouldn't you love to relax into the arms of the One who longs to bless you, to love you with a love that will never end, to fill you with all the fullness of Christ? Regardless of whether your circumstances change, your River Jordan evaporates? Wouldn't you love to unclench your iron fist of control, to unlock the shackles of your expectations, and walk forward in freedom?

What is stopping you?

The flooding Jordan River? The semi-arid land?

Your past? Your pre-programmed responses? Your painful earthly reminders of brokenness in your family? Your demands that God's answer look exactly as you expect rather than what He deems best?

Give it over. Get over yourself. Release your pain and brokenness, your disappointment and heartbreak, which have become your prison.

And ask your Daddy for a blessing. A blessing that He defines.

There is no flood too big, no desert too dry, to keep Him from loving you.

I can't wait to hear your laugh as you land in His arms. You will sound like a tinkling charm. And He will laugh with love and carry you through.

Travel Mercies

1. What situation in your life is less than ideal? What feels like a pre-arranged marriage where you had no choices? Maybe your marriage, your home, a prodigal child, a bad work environment. What are your default settings? Where do you automatically go to the "Woe is me" state of living, passively bemoaning your fate? How can you instead choose to live well in that place?

2. What is the terrain of your life like right now? If you are living in the semi-arid climate of the desert with a parched tongue and dehydrated soul, how will you live well? How will you quench your thirst, listen to your heart, and grow?

3. When have you longed to hear a blessing from someone? Who were you waiting for? What would you hope to hear from that person? If you directed those hopes toward God, who longs to give you the very best stored up for you, what would you ask? When have you asked and been disappointed? What did that do to your relationship with God?

4. What gift do you remember with delight from childhood, some surprise you weren't expecting from someone you loved? What about as an adult? When were you hoping for a gift and didn't receive it? How did you react? And when has God surprised you? When do you feel like an unloved child, not sensing God's delight and blessing?

5. When do you become an iron shackle rather than a tinkling anklet? What happens within you that creates that reaction? How can you work through that? Maybe, though, your problem is one of passivity: You sit back and hope and pray that someone will take care of you. How does that work? What would it look like for you to take an active role in your own life?

What Mean These Stones?

Write down a blessing for someone you love: your heart's desires for that person, your hopes, your pleasure in who they are. Invite God to create a place where you can give them that blessing.

Power Up

"Rejoice in the Lord always; again I will say, rejoice! Let your gentle spirit be known to all. . . . The Lord is near. Be anxious for nothing, but in everything by prayer and supplication with thanksgiving let your requests be made known to God. And the peace of God, which surpasses all comprehension, will guard your hearts and your minds in Christ Jesus. . . . And my God will supply all your needs according to His riches in glory in Christ Jesus."
—Philippians 4:4-7, 19 NASB

Rock-Hard Truth

"God's Word and His principles do offer a change-less blueprint for constructing or reconstructing relationships. A definition of the family blessing that contains five major elements reads:

A family blessing begins with *meaningful touching*. It continues with a *spoken message* of *high value*, a message that pictures a *special future* for the individual being blessed, and one that is based on an *active commitment* to see the blessing come to pass."
　—Gary Smalley and John Trent, PhD, *The Blessing* [20]

"In the biblical sense, if you give me your blessing, you irreversibly convey into my life not just something of the beneficent power and vitality of who you are, but something also of the life-giving power of God, in whose name the blessing is given."
　—Frederick Buechner, *Beyond Words* [21]

Remember Me, O Lord

Dear God,
I bless Your name.
Thank You for loving me.
Thank You for blessing me
with the hope and fullness of a life in Christ.
I put my heart's desires in Your hands;
please bring water to the arid land of my soul.
Set me free from expecting You
to look like I think You should look,
to act like I think You should act.
Let me relax in Your strong love
and trust You to care for me
as You deem best.
Because You love me,
I can trust You.
In Jesus' love.
Amen.

Memory Stone

For by grace
you have been saved through faith,
and that not of yourselves;
it is the gift of God,
not of works, lest anyone should boast.
For we are His workmanship,
created in Christ Jesus
for good works,
which God prepared beforehand that
we should walk in them.

— *Ephesians 2:8–10*

CHAPTER TEN

REMEMBERING AND STEPPING OUT

Kathryn lined up and followed other passengers onto her flight. Once in the air, her seatmate told some of her story: a Jewish woman and mother, highly intelligent, using her vacation to reconnect with extended family. She had abandoned her faith. After sharing her discouragement, the woman then said, "Tell me about you, Kathryn."

The Lord shoved at her heart, and Kathryn took a breath and explained about the ministry she helped run, a later-in-life venture that was occurring alongside her profession. What her Hebrew companion did not know, however, was that Kathryn's board of directors had just voted to sell their main ministry center, and all Kathryn really wanted to do was to quit both work and ministry and head home.

"What made you decide to start this avocation?"

Kathryn launched into her journey to salvation and God's overwhelming presence in her life. As she told her

*story, detailing each step of the way, Kathryn realized
again the clear leading of God.*

*She had boarded her plane disheartened at the latest
turn of events; she landed at her destination more con-
vinced than ever that God had a plan for her future, because He'd had a hand in her past.*

*Remembering God's guidance empowered her to take
the next step into the imminent unknown.*

*S*tepping into the Unknown

The women we have met in the Scriptures, the women whose
stories we have studied and whose lives we have listened to, all share
a common theme: they lived in a hard place, during hard times, and
God helped them move forward into their own unknown futures.
From Achsah to Zipporah, we see the Lord's hand propelling these
women forward, helping them face the challenges before them,
crossing their individual Jordan Rivers.

Without stories, we live impoverished lives. Stories of faith
build our faith, empowering us to engage in life even though life is
hard. Remembering our own stories helps us; and when we tell our
stories, others know they are not alone. Stacking our stones, sharing
our journeys, and offering vulnerable glimpses of our heart struggles
allow women to come along beside us. Our stories give others permission to be imperfect, permission to struggle, permission to question their own unknown futures.

When we remember with other women, our perspective changes.
Like Kathryn, we see where we have been: the twists, the turns, the
apparent detours and derailments. We see God's unmistakable hand
guiding the path our feet have trod. And sometimes we begin to see
why God allowed certain events: how one problem and its outworking prepared the way, or opened the door, to another new adventure
or a new growth place or a new relationship that changed the direction of our lives.

*L*isten

My mother has faithfully shared her stories throughout her life, and now her granddaughters, with children of their own, come sit at her feet and listen, listen. Afterward they will say to me, "I don't have anything to complain about after listening to Grandma's life." It isn't healthy to compare problems and disregard our own pain, but hearing another's journey offers us a balanced view of our own life and problems. Another's courage in a rock-hard place builds our faith and transfers courage to our own hearts.

Take time to listen to your life, to the lives of your extended family, to the lives of others around you, to God. And don't discount the value of the Jordan River you face this day. Listen to the waters rushing past and invite God to talk to you through them. As Virelle Kidder writes in *Donkeys Still Talk*, in a time of broken health for her entire family, with mounting sadness and financial problems,

> *I was haunted by the questions:* What would happen to our family? What would God allow next? *I still believed Christ died for my sins and lived in my heart, but the sadness over what He allowed made me wonder how much He really loved me.*
>
> *It never occurred to me then that God spoke in unexpected places and that the very problems I brought Him in prayer were often intended to carry me to a new listening place, straight into the presence of the God I so earnestly sought.*[22]

When we listen to our life, we run into God's presence. What is God trying to teach you through the flooded waters, the impassible rivers of your life? Perhaps He is inviting you in closer to His chest; inviting you in closer to your true self and your deepest longings. The invitation comes in odd containers, and the hard places of your life may be just the vehicle to convey you to His heart and help you to listen to His love song over you.

When Moses led the Israelites through the wilderness toward the Promised Land, he built a tent where he met with God. Whenever God's glory filled the tabernacle, the people of Israel stood still at the doorways of their tents, watching God's presence, listening intently.

Let God pull you to the doorway, where you stand and listen and watch for His brilliant presence. Let the very problems you encounter, the very issues that make you scream in frustration or retreat in depression, let those tug you to your tent flaps where you wait for God.

God has a plan for your future, because He's had a hand in your past.

And don't forget your hard places, where you lost sight of the fire by night and the cloud by day. Don't forget the darkness and the fear. Others need to hear your story, your lostness, your pain and grief and anxiety and despondency. They need to hear of the dark places in our lives. Parker Palmer writes,

> Many young people journey in the dark, as the young always have, and we elders do them a disservice when we withhold the shadowy parts of our lives. When I was young, there were very few elders willing to talk about the darkness; most of them pretended that success was all they had ever known. As the darkness began to descend on me in my early twenties, I thought I had developed a unique and terminal case of failure. I did not realize that I had merely embarked on a journey toward joining the human race.[23]

Remember those shadowy places. But remember too when the road straightens out and the waters roll back. Don't forget to remember where God has led you. God has a plan for your future, because He's had a hand in your past.

The Rearview Mirror

Stones of remembrance are like a spiritual diary, like looking in the rearview mirror while driving. You focus on the windshield in front of you, but glance in that rearview mirror to keep perspective. As we have looked back at these women's lives, we have also looked back at our own lives, observing where God's guidance appeared. In the rearview mirror we can see the pillar of cloud by day and the pillar of fire by night: the places where God watched over us, led us, protected us, redirected us.

Maybe you face forward and look at financial concerns. Look backward and see where God provided in the past. He is faithful. He did it before. He can do it again. Philippians 4:19 says, "And my God shall supply all your need according to His riches in glory by Christ Jesus." Those riches may not look exactly like we hope, but God is true to His Word. He will supply.

So look back, and lean forward.

Maybe you look ahead and worry about your children. They may be in diapers or they may be daddies and mommas already. Check your rearview mirror. Where did He help you along the way? Is He faithful? Can He do it again? Proverbs 22:6 reads, "Train up a child in the way he should go, and when he is old he will not depart from it." And though you have not been perfect as a parent, is God not the perfect parent? You have done your best; invite God to do the rest right alongside your efforts to love and raise your children from this day onward.

So look back, and lean forward.

Maybe you peer through the windshield and worry about your health, or the health of your loved ones. Look behind you—where has God been faithful? The Scriptures remind us, "For I am the Lord who heals you" (Exodus 15:26). We cannot dictate how that healing will look, but we know that if we ask for God's perfect will, He will answer in our best interest and for His glory.

So look back, and lean forward.

Maybe your worry is a job as you look ahead. Where have you seen God provide work in the past? This is our Jehovah Jireh, the God who provided a ram in the thicket to sacrifice when Abraham took his son Isaac to the mountain. God will provide. Didn't the psalmist say, "I have not seen the righteous forsaken, nor his descendants begging bread" (Psalms 37:25)?

So look back, and lean forward.

Maybe your windshield shows worries about your marriage; you have seen Him work in your marriage before. He can do it again. God made marriage; He can help you be the woman He desires in your marriage.

God is faithful to continue working in you, making you more holy as He is holy. "The One who called you is completely dependable. If he said it, he'll do it!" (1 Thessalonians 5:24 THE MESSAGE).

So look back, and lean forward.

We can look forward with anticipation to the crossing of our River Jordan, because we can look backward, see the stones of remembrance, and know that our God is faithful. "For I know the thoughts that I think toward you, says the Lord, thoughts of peace and not of evil, to give you a future and a hope" (Jeremiah 29:11).

Hold on to that future and hope, and listen to the Lord's words that follow: "Then you will call upon Me and go and pray to Me, and I will listen to you. And you will seek Me and find Me, when you search for Me with all your heart. I will be found by you, says the Lord, and I will bring you back from your captivity" (Jeremiah 29:12–14). God is faithful and findable.

Look back, and lean forward in hope. God promises a good future for you.

Look back, but not so long that you crash or park in life.

Look back, and lean forward.

Relying on the Word

Do you see the pattern? Look back, lean forward, and load up on the Word. Don't hike cross-country toward the Jordan without provisions! The only way God enables me to cross over my rivers has been to cling tightly to Him, stock up on Scriptures, and fill myself with God's Word. Jesus lived this out. When our Savior was in the wilderness being tempted by Satan, He didn't use a sword or knife or gun or some other weapon we might wield. He used the Word of God against every temptation the Devil tried to throw at Him.

If the living Word of God relied on the Word in the wilderness, no way will I attempt the rugged faith terrain and the flooding rivers of this earthly life without stockpiling the Word of God. "Let the Word of Christ dwell in you richly in all wisdom," says Paul in Colossians 3:16.

The River Jordan you face right now is *for your faith and future; it is also for others.*

But the Word doesn't stop there. We are not our own bottom line. The River Jordan you face right now *is* for your faith and future; it is also for others. So we stock up on Scripture for our own fortification, but also, Paul goes on to say, "teaching and admonishing *one another* in psalms and hymns and spiritual songs, singing with grace in your hearts to the Lord" (emphasis mine).

When the Lord told Joshua to "Take twelve stones" and build a memorial, He intended that others be encouraged in their journey as well. Our stories of faith are those stones of remembrance. They are our rearview mirrors, and our stories and our rich supply of God's Word stored up within us come out in a form that ministers to the people around us. We share our stories with others; we teach and admonish them; we sing, like Miriam, songs of grace and victory. We spill out God's goodness to others and to the Lord Himself.

Step Out

But, as we said in chapter 1, faith that does not act is faith that is just an act. We can't just remember. We can't just talk about what God has done and what God might do. We have to take the next step. Pick up our feet and walk. We have to "work it out." Philippians 2:12–15 reads,

Therefore, my beloved, as you have always obeyed, not as in my presence only, but now much more in my absence, work out your

own salvation with fear and trembling; for it is God who works in
you both to will and to do for His good pleasure.

Do all things without complaining and disputing, that you
may become blameless and harmless, children of God without
fault in the midst of a crooked and perverse generation, among
whom you shine as lights in the world. . . .

We work out our salvation by allowing God to work in us,
changing us, then working through us. It is a workout, a spiritual,
emotional, and sometimes physical exercise regime so that we can
grow strong in God's grace. This workout happens in the secret
place with God, and it works out in the midst of the chaotic and broken world around us.

We have to step out. Without grumbling or complaining, so that
we do not tarnish Christ's reputation. We have to move forward, by
faith, believing that God called us and God can deliver us. Believing
that if God says, "Take the land," we have to start walking. We work
it out by walking. Step out.

Like an exercise plan, don't sign up for a marathon when you
can't walk to the end of the block. Don't expect to take the land
overnight—take one step at a time, one footprint of faith at a time.

But take that first step. Life won't wait for you, and to wait is
deadly. Jesus said, "First things first. Your business is life, not death.
And life is urgent: Announce God's kingdom! . . . No procrastina-
tion. No backward looks. You can't put God's kingdom off till tomorrow. Seize the day" (Luke 9:60, 62 THE MESSAGE).

Take that step, even if circumstances don't make sense. Remember that when the Israelites reached the Jordan, it was flooded? They
had a hills-and-mountains situation. The leaders had to look to the
source of their strength to keep stepping, even in the flooded situation.
Joshua could have put it off because of the realities he faced. I would
have rationalized, "God didn't mean today. After all, it is flooded."

But until Joshua and the priests put their feet into the action,
nothing happened. When they stepped forward, then the waters
parted. So step forward!

We move from glory to glory, from victory to victory. In the
years between the Exodus and the settling of the Promised Land,

these women learned to trust the Lord more. "The Lord commanded," said the daughters of Zelophehad. In obedience the leaders
broke precedent and gave the women the land that the Lord commanded.

So start stepping. Walk it out. Work it out. One footprint of
faith at a time.

$\mathscr{T}$rust the Blesser

The working out of our faith, stepping forward into the land, requires obedience. And in rough terrain, obedience requires trust. We
have to trust the Blesser. God has a promise waiting for us as we
obey His word, as we trust Him and live a godly life, a bright life in a
dark world. If we walk, God does the rest. He tells us in Deuteronomy
28:1–9:

> Now it shall come to pass, if you diligently obey the voice of the
> Lord your God, to observe carefully all His commandments
> which I command you today, that the Lord your God will set you
> high above all nations of the earth. And all these blessings shall
> come upon you and overtake you, because you obey the voice of
> the Lord your God:
> Blessed shall you be in the city, and blessed shall you be in the
> country.
> Blessed shall be the fruit of your body, the produce of your
> ground and the increase of your herds, the increase of your cattle
> and the offspring of your flocks.
> Blessed shall be your basket and your kneading bowl.
> Blessed shall you be when you come in, and blessed shall you
> be when you go out.
> The Lord will cause your enemies who rise against you to be
> defeated before your face; they shall come out against you one
> way and flee before you seven ways.
> The Lord will command the blessing on you in your store-
> houses and in all to which you set your hand, and He will bless
> you in the land which the Lord your God is giving you.

The Lord will establish you as a holy people to Himself, just as He has sworn to you, if you keep the commandments of the Lord your God and walk in His ways.

Obedience is no magic formula. Job was more righteous than anyone on earth, and he still lost everything and everyone except his wife and some dubious friends. Yet God did not let him go, and eventually restored him.

The land may not look like much—yet. You aren't walking there—yet. But hold on:

> Though the fig tree may not blossom,
> Nor fruit be on the vines;
> Though the labor of the olive may fail,
> And the fields yield no food;
> Though the flock may be cut off from the fold,
> And there be no herd in the stalls—
> Yet I will rejoice in the Lord,
> I will joy in the God of my salvation.
> The Lord God is my strength;
> He will make my feet like deer's feet,
> And He will make me walk on my high hills.
> —Habakkuk 3:17–19

Though the Lord says that the land is owed us, that we have title to it, we must trust God enough to be obedient. We must trust the Blesser. He is the One who calls us forward.

Take the territory that God has promised, because He is not going to abandon you. In Joshua 1:5 the Lord says, "As I was with Moses, so I will be with you. I will not leave you nor forsake you." Do you hear that? "As I was with Moses." God is saying, "I have a history . . . I am the same yesterday, today, and forever. Be strong. You have My promise, My power, and My presence with you always."

God has a history, and wants us to walk out His story. He guarantees our success as long as we follow His plan for success. "This Book of the Law shall not depart from your mouth, but you shall meditate in it day and night." We're "to do according to all that is written" (Joshua 1:8).

James 1:22 reminds us, "But be ye doers of the word, and not hearers only, deceiving yourselves." You and I have to meditate to activate His promises in our lives fully and act by them.

And so we remember, and we walk.

Claim the Land

The challenges of our River Jordans—of life on this broken planet that is our home away from Home—are real but the gospel is true. We have to align the complexity of our problems with the simplicity of the gospel. If we do this God's way, we will step out of it. No one but He knows when that will be, but we can do our part. We can start walking. We can claim the land.

Problems today are severe and often secret; you alone know what goes on behind your closed doors. From bulimia to buyouts, from depression to drudgery, from abandonment to agoraphobia, from failure to unfaithfulness: there are no easy answers. We don't mean to imply that there are.

Yet there is no problem too large for God. You may not get the answers you expect. The river may take months or even years to recede in order for you to pass over. But there is no pit so deep that He is not deeper still. Learning to live in that place takes a sound support system, and deep time in God's presence. And a strong will to move into the Lord's promises.

It is no surprise that Caleb's daughter Achsah demonstrated such determination. Like father, like daughter. Caleb was forty years old when he first surveyed the Promised Land, when he first stood for God's promises and was willing to claim what the Lord had deeded the Israelites. Nearly four decades later, we find him finally on the right side of the promise.

With vigor he reminds the people of Moses' words to him, "So Moses swore on that day, saying, 'Surely the land where your foot has trodden shall be your inheritance and your children's forever, because you have wholly followed the Lord my God'" (Joshua 14:9).

He wraps up his presentation with words that shame our youth-worshiping culture:

> "And now, behold, the Lord has kept me alive, as He said, these forty-five years, ever since the Lord spoke this word to Moses while Israel wandered in the wilderness; and now, here I am this day, eighty-five years old. As yet I am as strong this day as on the day that Moses sent me; just as my strength was then, so now is my strength for war, both for going out and for coming in. Now therefore, give me this mountain of which the Lord spoke in that day. . . ." (Joshua 14:10–12)

Age has no bearing in God's sight, except that as we age we (hopefully) grow in wisdom and experience and maturity. Caleb maintained his original vision: he remembered the Promised Land and stayed strong and fit to claim it himself. You may be eighty-five when you take the land—or you may be eighteen! But take it you must. It has been deeded to you, the Land of Promise, the land of God's presence. Can you say with Caleb, "Now give me this mountain"?

The river you can't cross, the problem you can't solve, the relationship you can't fix: can you say, "Now give me this mountain"?

The floods you can't ford, the focus you can't find, the failure you can't eradicate: can you say, "Now give me this mountain"?

The sand you can't shake, the tent you can't stake, the rope you can't break: can you say, "Now give me this mountain"?

Now therefore, give me this mountain of which the Lord spoke in that day. . . ."

Claim your Mountain
Claim your Passion
Claim your Life
Claim your Ministry
Claim your Goals

Claim your Hopes
Claim your Dreams
Take this Day
Take this Step
Say with Caleb, "Give me this mountain!"
Will it be easy? No.
Will it be automatic? No.
Will it be immediate? No.

But when we move toward the mountain, we move toward God. We move with God. And perhaps, after all, that is the point of the mountain.

Wait, though. Before you step out, take off your shoes. Like Joshua before you, and Moses before him, hear the Lord say to you, "Take your sandal off your foot, for the place where you stand is holy."

It is tempting to believe that once we cross over, we're on holy ground. But no. The place where you stand today *is* the holy place. The river you can't cross, the mountain you can't scale, the rocks you can't move: This is holy ground.

So please. Take off your shoes.

You're standing on holy ground.

Remember where you have been. Where you are. And then, start steppin'.

Travel Mercies

1. As we have journeyed with the women in Scripture, whose story has most resonated with you? What is God trying to teach you through the flooded waters, the impassable rivers? As you look through the windshield, what do you see in the rearview mirror of your life?

2. Where is it hardest to listen? To others' stories? To your own heart and story? To God's whispered words? Why? When have you refused to listen and stayed stuck, or moved forward

on your own agenda and timing rather than God's? When have you listened and been empowered to move forward?

3. What does it look like for you to work out your salvation in fear and trembling? Where do the fear and trembling come in? How hard is obedience for you? When do you feel lost in a dark and polluted world, rather than someone shining like a light? What contributes to that feeling?

4. Where are your biggest struggles to "trust the Blesser"? What does obedience look like in this rock-hard place? Looking back, where have you found God's faithfulness building your faith into a rock-hard testimony of His goodness?

5. Describe what it means to you to "Claim this mountain."

What Mean These Stones?

How you live in history will determine how you live in eternity. What memorial are you building? Are you stacking stones that glorify God? Or a disheveled pile of rocks that bears no resemblance to the Lord's glory working in your life and heart? What stories will you tell your children and your children's children and all who pass by your life who ask you, "What mean these stones?"

Power Up

When I was living among you, you lived in responsive obedience. Now that I'm separated from you, keep it up. Better yet, redouble your efforts. Be energetic in your life of salvation, reverent and sensitive before God. That energy is God's energy, an energy deep within you, God himself willing and working at what will give him the most pleasure.

Do everything readily and cheerfully—no bickering, no second-guessing allowed! Go out into the world uncorrupted, a

breath of fresh air in this squalid and polluted society. Provide
people with a glimpse of good living and of the living God.
—*Philippians* 2:12-15 THE MESSAGE

Rock-Hard Truth

"We will never find enough of God at any single
place of prayer to satisfy us long. Why? Because he
moves! We, too, must journey, ever following the ark,
ever holding on to God as we journey toward him. We
travel toward him for two reasons. First, we will find all
of him someday at that glorious place where life's journey ends. But second, as we travel toward him, the journey itself brings him near. Jesus is the Emmaus Christ
(Luke 24:13) who both walks us along the journey and
reveals himself to us at the journey's end."
—Calvin Miller, *The Unchained Soul*

Remember Me, O Lord

Lord God:
You lead me on a journey
through hot desert and flooding waters.
But You have promised that
"The rivers of woe shall not thee overflow."
And so, this day, I choose to trust You.
Even though this river is high,
I choose to say,
"You are good. You are faithful."
I say with those who have gone before me,
"You are good. You are faithful."

*I look in the rearview mirror of my life
and see that
"You are good. You are faithful."
And I choose.
I choose to step forward
and claim this land.
And then I find
You.
Life is hard.
But You are good.
Thank You. Bless You.
In Jesus' name.
Amen.*

Notes

1. Charles Spurgeon, *Daily Help* (New York: Grosset & Dunlap, January 5, year unknown), 5. Spurgeon's original spelling of "unctuous" was "unctious."

2. *Strong's Exhaustive Concordance.*

3. Catherine Clark Kroeger and Mary J. Evans, eds., *The IVP Women's Bible Commentary* (Downers Grove, Ill.: InterVarsity, 2002), 286.

4. Terrence Des Pres, *The Survivor* (Oxford University Press, 1976), 162, as quoted by Philip Yancey in *Open Windows* (Westchester, Ill.: Good News, 1982), 15.

5. Yancey, *Open Windows*, 16.

6. J. Otis Ledbetter, *In the Secret Place* (Sisters, Ore.: Multnomah, 2003), 36.

7. Jennifer Kennedy Dean, executive director, The Praying Life Foundation.

8. As told on Joyce Meyer's television ministry.

9. Spurgeon, *Daily Help* (December 11), 176.

10. Karen Mains, *The God Hunt* (Downers Grove, Ill.: InterVarsity, 2003), 13.

11. John H. Walton, Victor H. Matthews, and Mark W. Chavalas, *The IVP Bible Background Commentary: Old Testament* (Downers Grove, Ill.: InterVarsity, 2000), 79.

12. "Lovely Ladies," lyrics by Herbert Kretzmer, music by Alain Boubil and Claude-Michel Schonberg, ©1987 The David Geffen Company.

13. From a phone interview with Gretta Wilson, Genesis House, Chicago, 1/16/06.

14. "In a survey of non-violent female offenders in Cook County Jail, 80% had a history of involvement in prostitution. Of these incarcerated, 81% have children, who often must be cared for by the State while their mothers are in prison."

15. http://www.thetimesonline.com/articles/2005/04/13/news/illiana/0d38b8c40d70e5cc86256fe1007f5f6b.prt.

16. For more on abandonment, please see *Resting Place: A Personal Guide to Spiritual Retreat* by Jane Rubietta (Downers Grove, Ill.: InterVarsity, 2005), chapter 3.

17. *Indeed* magazine, © Jane Rubietta, 2006.

18. George MacDonald, *Unspoken Sermons (Series One)* (London: Alexander Strahan, 1867), 24; and *Unspoken Sermons (Series Two)* (London: Longmans, Green, & Co., 1895), 74; both as quoted in *George MacDonald, Selections from His Greatest Works*, compiled by David L. Neuhouser (Wheaton, Ill.: SP Publications, 1990), 19. MacDonald's original spelling of "fullness" was "fulness."

19. Dr. Bruce H. Wilkinson, *The Prayer of Jabez: Breaking Through to the Blessed Life* (Sisters, Ore.: Multnomah, 2000), 23–24.

20. Gary Smalley and John Trent, PhD, *The Blessing* (Nashville, Tenn.: Nelson, 1986), 19, 24.

21. Frederick Buechner, *Beyond Words: Daily Readings in the ABC's of Faith* (New York: HarperCollins, 2004), 48.

22. Virelle Kidder, *Donkeys Still Talk: Hearing God's Voice When You're Not Listening* (Colorado Springs: NavPress, 2004), 20.

23. Parker J. Palmer, *Let Your Life Speak: Listening for the Voice of Vocation* (San Francisco: Jossey-Bass, 2000), 18–19.

Seasons of a Woman's Life

Lois Evans

Lois Evans, through the life of Esther, walks women through the seasons of seed planting, growth, and harvest in their lives. She encourages them to enjoy the changing seasons and hold fast to the promises of God.

Paperback
ISBN: 0-8024-8592-8
ISBN-13: 978-0-8024-8592-2

MOODY
PUBLISHERS

THE NAME YOU CAN TRUST®
www.MoodyPublishers.com

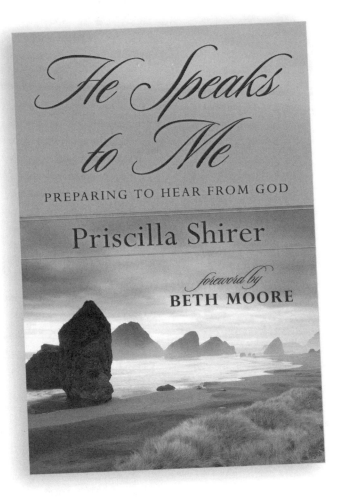

He Speaks to Me
Preparing to Hear From God

Priscilla Shirer

Priscilla Shirer speaks directly to the need to develop a richer prayer life and a deeper, more intimate relationship with God. Based on the life of Samuel, who first heard God's voice when he was a little boy, this book will help readers learn how to comfortably share their experiences with God and hear from Him in more practical ways.

Paperback
ISBN: 0-8024-5007-5
ISBN-13: 978-0-8024-5007-4

MOODY
PUBLISHERS

THE NAME YOU CAN TRUST®
www.MoodyPublishers.com